IN THE PRESENCE OF MY FATHER

PRAYERS FROM THE BIBLE

IN THE PRESENCE
OF MY FATHER

PRAYERS FROM THE BIBLE

Translated and compiled by
LAURENCE BRETT

HELICON
Baltimore

Helicon Press, Inc.
1120 N. Calvert Street
Baltimore, Maryland 21202

Library of Congress Catalog Card Number 67–13788

Printed in the United States of America

Contents

5

3. GOD

THE FATHER

THE SON

THE HOLY SPIRIT

4. THE CHURCH

5. THE CHRISTIAN

6. REPENTANCE AND FORGIVENESS

7. SUPPLICATIONS

8. PRAYERS

9. INTERCESSIONS

10. THANKSGIVINGS

ABBREVIATIONS

Gen—Genesis
Ex—Exodus
Lev—Leviticus
Num—Numbers
Deut—Deuteronomy
Josh—Joshua
Judg—Judges
Ruth—Ruth
1 Sam—1 Samuel (1 Kings)
2 Sam—2 Samuel (2 Kings)
1 Kings—1 Kings (3 Kings)
2 Kings—2 Kings (4 Kings)
1 Chron—1 Chronicles
　　　(1 Paralipomenon)
2 Chron—2 Chronicles
　　　(2 Paralipomenon)
Ezra—Ezra (1 Esdras)
Neh—Nehemiah (2 Esdras)
Tob—Tobit (Tobias)
Judith—Judith
Esther—Esther
Job—Job
Ps—Psalms
Prov—Proverbs
Eccles—Ecclesiastes (Qoheleth)

Song—Song of Solomon
　　　(Canticle of Canticles)
Wis—Wisdom of Solomon
　　　(Wisdom)
Sir—Sirach (Ecclesiasticus)
Is—Isaiah
Jer—Jeremiah
Lam—Lamentations
Bar—Baruch
Ezek—Ezekiel
Dan—Daniel
Hos—Hosea (Osee)
Joel—Joel
Amos—Amos
Obad—Obadiah (Abdias)
Jon—Jonah
Mic—Micah (Micheas)
Nahum—Nahum
Hab—Habakkuk
Zeph—Zephaniah (Sophonias)
Hag—Haggai (Aggeus)
Zech—Zechariah (Zacharias)
Mal—Malachi (Malachias)
1 Mac—1 Maccabees
2 Mac—2 Maccabees

Mt—Matthew
Mk—Mark
Lk—Luke
Jn—John
Acts—Acts of the Apostles
Rom—Romans
1 Cor—1 Corinthians
2 Cor—2 Corinthians
Gal—Galatians
Eph—Ephesians
Phil—Philippians
Col—Colossians
1 Thess—1 Thessalonians
2 Thess—2 Thessalonians

1 Tim—1 Timothy
2 Tim—2 Timothy
Tit—Titus
Philem—Philemon
Heb—Hebrews
Jas—James
1 Pet—1 Peter
2 Pet—2 Peter
1 Jn—1 John
2 Jn—2 John
3 Jn—3 John
Jude—Jude
Rev—Apocalypse
Ap—Apocrypha

Introduction

BY LAURENCE BRETT

Why a book of prayers? Because many of us today have almost forgotten how to pray, and are beginning to wonder if prayer itself is irrelevant. There is so much we ought to do to promote justice and peace, and such a great need for genuine concern and care, that the emphasis really should be upon involvement. Fortunately we have begun to learn one lesson: such involvement is itself a prayer, and our worship is sterile unless it leads to works of love for others.

But it is equally true that our efforts are not the only form of prayer, and the Christian, like the Lord he follows, must "go apart" from time to time and speak with his Father. It is as much a distortion to forget about prayer and only "do something," as it is to relinquish our duty to our fellow man in favor of escaping into quiet corners for prayer. A balanced outlook considers our worship and our work as being both essential; we are no more apart from God when we are with men, than we are apart from men when we draw closer to God in prayer.

To help restore this balance, to offer some sources of godliness to the man who goes "where the action is" and to persuade those who only want to pray that involvement is needed—this is the purpose of this book.

Why, then, a book of prayers from the Bible? There are many reasons. The Scriptures reveal God's own thoughts about himself, and some of man's deepest thoughts about both himself and his God, and prayer tells us as much about our own selves as it does about the God within us. Christ prayed the Psalms at various stages of his ministry, and even upon the cross. What is perhaps important for us to remember is that the Scriptures, in Alcuin's words, form "the table of Christ, from which we are nourished, from which we learn what we should love and hope for, and to whom we should have our eyes raised."

If members of the various Christian Churches can be nourished from this, their common table, then there is great hope that one day they will "break bread together" at the table of the Lord's Supper. For too long a time have Christians lived and loved separately, and refused to explore together what they held in common. We have too much to offer each other to let that attitude continue. This book of prayers was drawn from the Bible with the hope that all Christians can use it when they pray to the one "God and Father of us all." And if, as is possible, some will not be able to use all the prayers, then perhaps they will use what their personal convictions will allow.

In choosing a prayer, the reader will be guided by his own needs and feelings: the mother awaiting the delivery of her child will want to pray for the safety and health of all her children, and the safe delivery of this latest child; people living in cities torn by riots and racism will feel the need to call upon God for peace; the assassination of a great man, such as John F. Kennedy and Dr. Martin Luther King, Jr., will be the occasion of a prayer in time of great sorrow, or a prayer of repentance; the common moments of depression and elation that beset us all will present their own needs for prayer, and the selections contained here are meant for every time and season of the soul.

There are four types of prayer, depending upon the nature of the text itself. The first is composed of passages that appear as prayers within the Bible itself, such as the Lord's own prayer, or the Canticle of Simeon. The second type are passages that only had to be adapted to become a prayer; thus, for example, Paul's famous hymn on the attributes of love becomes a prayer when we ask God to show us this "more excellent way." The third type is composed of various verses taken from the many books of the Bible; the Prayer for Peace uses phrases from the Old and New Testaments, symbolic, so it seems, of man's endless quest for peace.

The last type of prayer uses a scriptural text, followed by a prayer from one of the Christian traditions which seems to complete the text, and which serves as a commentary upon God's Word. This last type points out how indebted we are to the Scriptures for showing us how to pray; and so only a few have been included, with the hope that the reader will himself try to uncover, within the Bible, the source of his own favorite prayers. Also, because the Psalter is widely used as a manual of prayers, and because there are many excellent translations available, only a small number of Psalms have been included.

Lastly, something should be said about the translation of the biblical passages themselves. Many of the texts were not intended as prayers, but only as admonitions, suggestions, or simple statements of faith. Because they take on new and deeper insights when used as prayers, I decided to translate them afresh, and, in some cases (indicated by the use of italics), to give them a different direction. In most cases I retained the words that would be familiar to the reader of the Bible, so that he could recall the context in which they were originally used. I do not mean to imply that the Scriptures are in need of improvement, but only that a new approach to the Scriptures as prayer demands a different way of looking at the texts; besides, God's Word was intended for our use, to ponder and make our own, to speak freely just as they were so freely given us as God's own children.

1. *Prayer*

IN GOD'S PRESENCE

I am here! I come	PS 40:7
into the presence of God,	
who gives life to all things;	I TIM 6:13
in the presence of my Father	
and his angels,	REV 3:5
in the presence of the holy angels	
and in the presence of the Lamb,	REV 14:10
the presence of the Son of Man;	LK 21:36
for in your presence	
is the fullness of joy,	PS 16:11
and the upright	
shall dwell in your presence.	PS 140:13

I PRAY

I *pray* to the God of my life,   PS 42:8
  pure prayers to God   JOB 16:18
  to give glory in prayer;   NEH 11:17

I *pray* to the Father,   MT 6:6
  that the Lord may fulfill his word,   I SAM 1:23
  and in the Holy Spirit;   JUDE 20

I *pray* always,   MK 18:1
  continually,   ACTS 6:4
  without ceasing;   ACTS 12:5
  in the morning,   PS 88:13
  evening, morning and noon,   PS 55:17
  before you now, night and day;   NEH 1:6

I *pray* in this place,   2 CHRON 7:15
  in every place;   I TIM 2:8
  alone,   LK 9:18
  in the company of the faithful,
    in the assembly;   PS 111:1
  with fasting,   ACTS 14:22
  with many prayers;   2 MAC 12:24

I *pray* for those who persecute or slander,   MT 5:44
  forgiving whatever I have against anyone;   MT 11:25

I *pray* the prayer of the poor man,   PS 102:1
  the prayer of one in need,   PS 102:17
  the prayer of the just,   PROV 15:29
  the prayer of faith.   JAS 5:15

THE PRAYER OF EZRA

Lord, who lives for ever,
    whose eyes are exalted,
    whose upper chambers are the heavens,
    whose throne is beyond measure,
    whose glory is beyond limit,
before whom armies of angels tremble,
  at whose bidding
    they are changed to wind and fire,
    whose word is sure,
    whose utterances certain,
    whose orders stand firm,
    whose commands inspire awe,
    whose glance drives the ocean depths,
    whose anger melts mountains,
  and whose truth can never change,
Lord,
hear your servant's prayer,
heed your creature's request,
listen to my words. Amen.   AP 2 ESD 8:20–24

THE PRAYER OF SARAH

You are blessed,
Lord, God of mercy!
Blessed is your name,
holy,
honored forever!
May all your works praise you,
forever!
    And now, Lord,
    I have turned my eyes
    and my gaze,
    towards you.   TOB 3:11-12

THE PRAYER OF PAUL

I will pray with the spirit,
and with the mind as well.
I will sing praise,
    with the spirit,
and with the mind as well.   I COR 14:15

FROM THE PSALTER

Sing to the Lord, all the earth!
Serve God with gladness,
come into his presence with songs of joy!

Know that the Lord is God,
he made us, and we are his—
his people, the flock he tends.

Come in through his gates with thanks,
through his courts with praise;
give him praise, and bless his name!

Yes, the Lord is good;
his love is lasting,
his faithfulness is from age to age.   PS 100

Lord, let my prayer come in before you,
    let your word bring me perception.

May my requests reach your presence,
    rescue me as you have promised.

May my lips speak out your praise,
    since you teach me your commands.   PS 119:169-171

A DOXOLOGY

Glory to him
who can keep *us* from falling,
 and bring *us* safe
into his glorious presence
without blemish
and with rejoicing.

To God,
the only God,
who saves us
through Jesus Christ our Lord,
be glory,
 majesty,
 authority and
 power,
which was his before time began,
is now,
and shall be for ever. Amen.

JUDE 24–25

2. Of Times and Seasons

THE SACREDNESS OF TIME

For everything there is a season,
and a time for every matter under heaven:
A time to be born, and a time to die;
a time to plant, and a time to uproot what is planted.

A time to kill, and a time to heal;
a time to tear down, and a time to build.
A time to weep, and a time to laugh;
a time to mourn, and a time to dance.

A time to throw stones away,
      and a time to gather them;
a time to embrace, and a time to refrain from embracing.
A time to seek, and a time to lose;
a time to keep, and a time to throw away.

A time to tear, and a time to sew;
a time to keep still, and a time to speak.
A time to love, and a time to hate;
a time for war, and a time for peace.

Everything *you* do is apt for its time;
you have placed the timeless into *our* hearts,
without man's ever discovering,
from beginning to end,
the work which God has done.   ECCLES 3:1–8,11 (ADAPTED)

THE PRAYER OF THE HOURS

AT DEAD OF NIGHT
> you were born for us and our salvation;
> may we be daily born again,
> till Christ be fully formed in us, and
> SAVE US!

EARLY IN THE MORNING,
> the sun yet arising, you rose from the dead;
> raise us up daily to new life,
> suggesting ways of repentance, and
> SAVE US!

AT THE THIRD HOUR
> you sent your Spirit upon the Apostles;
> take not your Holy Spirit from us,
> but renew him within us, and
> SAVE US!

AT THE SIXTH HOUR
> you nailed our sins with your body on the cross;
> blot out the handwriting of our sins,
> taking it away, and
> SAVE US!

AT THE SEVENTH HOUR
> you bade the fever leave the nobleman's son;
> remove whatever is of sickness
> or fever within us, and
> SAVE US!

AT THE NINTH HOUR
> you tasted death for us sinners and our sins;
> put to death within us
> whatever is contrary to your will, and
> SAVE US!

AT THE TENTH HOUR
  your Apostle cried, "We have found the Messiah!";
  grant us always to find you
  with like rejoicing, and
  SAVE US!
AT EVENTIDE
  you willed to be taken from the cross and buried;
  bury our sins,
  enshrouding our guilt within your loving-kindness, and
  SAVE US!
AT SUPPER TIME
  you set forth the mysteries of your Body and Blood;
  make us mindful of them,
  and partakers unto forgiveness, and
  SAVE US!
AT MIDNIGHT
  you awakened Paul, as you had David,
                                  to sing your praises;
  give us songs by night,
  and to remember you upon our beds, and
  SAVE US!
AT AN HOUR YET UNKNOWN
  you shall come to judge us!
  in every hour and day,
  prepare us for your gracious advent, and
  SAVE US!   BASED ON A PRAYER OF LANCELOT ANDREWES

The Day

GOD'S EVER-PRESENT LOVE

The loyal love of the Lord never ends,
his kindnesses are not spent;
they are new every morning,
so great is your faithfulness.

"The Lord is my portion," says my soul,
"and so I will hope in him."
The Lord is good to those who trust him,
    to the soul that seeks him.
It is good to wait quietly
for the saving help of the Lord.   LAM 3:22–25

A MORNING PRAYER

Lord,
the day belongs to you;   PS 25:5
the night is far gone,
the day is at hand;   ROM 13:12
let us cast off the works of darkness,
Lord,
and put on light for armor;
let us conduct ourselves fittingly,
as in the day;   ROM 13:13
since we belong to the day,
let us be alert,
wearing faith and love for a shield,
and the hope of salvation for a helmet.

Through our Lord Jesus Christ
who died for us,
so that, whether we wake or sleep,
we might live with him.   I THESS 5:8,10

PRAYER OF ISAIAH

Lord, be gracious to us;
we hope in you.
Be our strength each morning,
our salvation in time of trouble.   IS 33:2

PRAYER OF JUDITH

Give me strength, this day,
Lord, God of Israel!   JUDITH 13:7

AN OFFERING OF OUR DAY

You are my Rock, my Fortress;
for your name's sake guide me,
    lead me!

Draw me out of the net
    they have spread for me,
for you are my Refuge;
Into your hands I commit my spirit,
for you have redeemed me, Lord.   PS 31:3-5

Into your hands this day, Lord God,
we commit ourselves,
    and all who are dear to us.
Let the gift of your special presence
be with us even to its close.

Grant us never to lose sight of you
    all day long,
but to worship and pray to you,
that at eventide we may again
    give thanks to you.
Through Christ our Lord. Amen.

GELASIAN SACRAMENTARY

LIVING IN THE LIGHT

The night is over,
the real light is already shining.
Anyone who claims to be in the light
but hates his brother
is still in the dark.
Anyone who loves his brother
lives in the light,
and has no fear of stumbling.   1 JN 2:8-10

Lord Jesus Christ,
the world's true Sun
     ever rising,
     never setting,
whose life-giving warmth
     engenders,
     preserves,
     nourishes and
     gladdens
all things in heaven or earth,
shine into my soul, I pray.

Scatter the night of sin,
     and the clouds of error.

Blaze within me,
that I may go my way without stumbling,
taking no part in the shameful deeds
     that men do in darkness,
but all my life long
walking as one native to the Light. Amen.   ERASMUS

FOR CONTINUAL DAY

God, *You* chose what is foolish in the world
    to shame the wise;
You chose what is weak in the world,
    to shame the strong; and
You chose what is common
    and contemptible in the world,
those who are nothing,
to shame those who are "everything,"
so that no man might boast
in the presence of God.   I COR 1:27–29

Lord God,
You have chosen the weak things in the world,
    to confound the mighty,
shed continual day upon us who watch for you;
that our lips may praise you,
    our life may bless you,
and our meditations give you glory. Amen   SARUM BREVIARY

TO THE LORD OF DAY AND NIGHT

You are Master over night and day,
you fixed the sun and its light;   PS 74:16
you make both dawn and dark   AMOS 4:13
and turn dusk to dawn;   5:8
in your sight,
the world is like a morning dew,
that quickly passes away.   WIS 11:22

I am up before dawn to call for help,   PS 119:147
for you will come to us
    as certain as the dawn,   HOS 6:3
and I sing of your love
    morning after morning;   PS 59:16
to those who are victorious,
who work for *you* to the end,
give *your* Morning Star.   REV 2:28

FROM THE PSALTER

Listen to my words, Lord,
    heed my sighing.
Hear my prayer for help,
    my King, and my God!
I pray to you, Lord,
    at daybreak you hear my voice;
at dawn I bring my plea
    hopefully before you.   PS 5:1-3

My heart is ready, God,
my heart is steadfast;
    I will sing and chant praise!
Awake, my soul!
awake, lyre and harp;
    I will wake the dawn!
Lord, I will praise you among the peoples,
    I will sing your praise among nations,
For your love is high as heaven,
    your faithfulness above the clouds!

Rise high above all heavens, God,
  raise your glory above the earth!
—to bring help to those who love you,
help us with your right hand, and save us! ps 108:1–5

BEFORE THE DAY'S WORK

Let your work be seen by your servants,
and your glorious power by their children.
Let the favor of the Lord our God be ours,
  and prosper the work of our hands.
Yes, prosper the work of our hands. ps 90:16–17

Lord God, King of heaven and earth,
be pleased this day
  to direct and make holy,
  to guide and govern,
  our hearts and bodies,
  our thoughts, words and deeds,
in accord with your law,
and the keeping of your commands;
that now and forever
we may, with your help,
be saved and set free;
Savior of the world,
who live and reign forever. Amen. roman breviary

PRAYER FOR GROWTH

A blessing on the man
who does not follow the advice
    of evil men;
he is like a tree
    planted near running waters,
that yields its fruit in season,
    whose leaves never wither.   PS 1:1 & 3

Lord Jesus,
grant me to give you
    my whole being,
tree and fruit alike,
the finished work
as well as the harnessed power.   TEILHARD DE CHARDIN

DOXOLOGY

To him,
whose power working within us
can do immeasurably more
than we can ask or even imagine,
to him
be the glory,
    in the Church,
    and in Jesus Christ,
through all generations
forever and ever. Amen   EPH 3:20-21

BEFORE UNDERTAKING ANY STUDY

If you want wisdom, keep the commandments,
    and the Lord will grant her to you.
For wisdom and study mean the fear of the Lord,
    and meekness and faithfulness please him.   SIR 1:25–26

Your pleasure, merciful God—
grant that I may
    desire it ardently,
    learn it carefully,
    recognize it truly,
    fulfill it perfectly,
to the praise and glory of your name.

Lord my God,
give me
    an understanding that knows you,
    a diligence that seeks you,
    a wisdom that finds you,
    a way of life that pleases you,
    a steadfastness that waits for you,
    and a confidence that shall at last embrace you.
ST. THOMAS AQUINAS

PRAYER OF SOLOMON

May God grant me
to speak as he would wish,
and express thoughts
worthy of what I have received.
For he is the guide of Wisdom,
and he directs the wise.
Both we
    and our works
are in his hand,
as are all our understanding
    and skill in doing.   WIS 7:15–16

PRAYER AT EVENING

Of old you established the earth,
    and the heavens are the work of your hands.
They will perish, but you will remain;
    they shall wear out like a garment.
Like clothing, you change them, and they are changed,
    but you are the same, your years without end.
                      PS 102:26-28

Be present, most merciful God,
    and protect us
through the silent hours of this night,
so that we who are wearied
by the changes and chances of this world
may take rest in your abiding changelessness.
Through Christ our Lord. Amen.   ST. AMBROSE

PRAYER OF ST. AUGUSTINE

God, *you* have not destined us for *your* wrath,
but to obtain salvation,
  through our Lord, Jesus Christ,
  who died for us,
so that, whether awake or asleep,
we might live with him.   I THESS 5:9–10

Dear Lord,
watch with those
who wake,
  or watch,
  or weep tonight,
and give your angels charge
  over all who sleep.

Tend your sick ones, Lord Christ;
rest your weary ones,
bless your dying ones,
soothe your suffering ones,
pity your afflicted ones,
shield your joyous ones,
and all for your love's sake. Amen. ST. AUGUSTINE

TOWARDS EVENING

Man goes out to his work,
to labor until evening;   PS 104:23
Lord, what variety you have fashioned,
arranging things in wisdom.   104:24

Lord, I call to you now, hurry to me,
    listen to me, as I call upon you.
Let my prayer rise like incense,
    the lifting of my hands
    like an evening sacrifice.   PS 141:1–2

A day is yet to come—
    it will be a day of wonder,
with no changing of day to night,
    and full light in the evening;   ZECH 14:6–7
Lord, you have blessed the evening,
for in the evening,
they brought to him, *your Son,*
all who were sick,
or possessed by devils,
—and he cured many sufferers.   MK 1:32–33

Therefore, Lord,
be with us,
for it is getting towards evening now,
and the day is almost over.   LK 24:28

THE CANTICLE OF SIMEON

Now, Master, you can let your servant go
   —in peace, as you have promised;
for my eyes have seen the salvation
     which you have prepared
     for all nations to see,
a light—to enlighten the pagans,
     and to add lustre to your people, Israel.   LK 2:29–32

The Week

COMMEMORATION OF EASTER, FOR SUNDAY

On the first day of the week,
at early dawn,
they went to the tomb,
taking the spices they had prepared.
And they found the stone
    rolled away from the tomb,
but when they went in,
they did not find the body.   LK 24:1-3

V. The Lord has risen from the tomb. Alleluia!
R. Who for our sins hung upon the tree. Alleluia!
Let us pray.
In honor of the Lord's Day,
the beginning of our Resurrection,
let us unite our hearts
and offer fitting praise
    to the Holy One, our God;
begging his mercy
that he will grant us to be
partakers, body and soul,
in the blessed Resurrection
of our Lord and Savior,
who lives and reigns forever and ever. Amen.
        ANCIENT ROMAN PRAYER

FOR THE DAYS OF THE WEEK

SUNDAY

Lord, you spoke when creation began,
and on the first day, said,
"Let heaven and earth be made!"
and your word accomplished the work.
Then was the Spirit hovering,
and darkness and quiet embraced all things;
the sound of man's voice was not yet there.
Then it was that you commanded a ray of light
be brought forth from your treasuries,
that your works might then appear.

All this have I spoken before you, Lord,
for you said that it was for us
that you have made this world.   AP 2 ESD 6:38-40
                                                      6:55

MONDAY

Again, on the second day,
you formed the spirit of the heavens,
and ordered him
to divide and separate the waters,
that one part might move upwards,
and the other remain below.

All this have I spoken before you, Lord,
for you have said that it was for us
that you have made this world.   AP 2 ESD 6:41   6:55

On the third day
you ordered the waters to gather together
in the seventh part of the earth;
six parts you dried up,
that some of them might be planted
    and cared for,
and be of service before you.
Your Word went forth,
and at once your work was done.
Immediately, fruit appeared
    in endless richness,
with appeal to various tastes;
    flowers appeared,
    in unmatchable colors;
    and sweet smells,
    beyond our power to describe;
these were made on the third day.

All this have I spoken before you, Lord,
for you said that it was for us
that you have made this world.   AP 2 ESD 6:42–44 6:55

WEDNESDAY

On the fourth day,
you commanded the brightness of the sun,
    the light of the moon,
    and the arrangement of the stars
to come into being;
you commanded them to be of service to man,
who was then about to be formed.

All this have I spoken before you, Lord,
for you said that it was for us
that you have made this world.   AP 2 ESD 6:45–46
                                             6:55

THURSDAY

On the fifth day
you commanded the seventh part,
    where the waters were gathered,
to bring forth living creatures,
    birds and fishes;
and so it was done.
The still and lifeless water
produced creatures that live,
as it was ordered,
that nations might therefore
declare your wondrous works.

All this have I spoken before you, Lord,
for you said that it was for us
that you have made this world.   AP 2 ESD 6:47–48
                                             6:55

FRIDAY

On the sixth day
you commanded the earth
to bring forth before you,
    cattle,
    beasts,
    and creeping things;
and over these you placed Adam,
ruler of all the works you made;
from him have we all come,
the people you have chosen.

All this have I spoken before you, Lord,
for you said that it was for us
that you have made this world.   AP 2 ESD 6:53-54
                                      6:55

SATURDAY

The heavens and earth were done,
and all their array.
On the seventh day, God, *you* rested
from all the work *you* had done.
You blessed this seventh day,
    making it holy,
for on it *you* rested
from all the work of creation.

All this have I spoken before you, Lord,
for you said that it was for us
that you have made this world.   GEN 2:1-3
                                 AP 2 ESD 6:55

The Year

ADVENT PRAYER

Heavens, shower from above,
and let the skies rain down
    righteousness.
Let the earth open
for salvation to spring up,
and let deliverance bud forth. IS 45:8

ANCIENT PRAYER

You must be patient,
and not lose heart,
for the Lord's coming is near!

Do not carry grudges against each other,
so as not to be brought to judgment yourselves;
the Judge can already be seen at the gates. JAS 5:8-9

Graciously hear your people's prayers, Lord,
that we who rejoice at the coming in the flesh
    of your only-begotten Son
may receive
when he comes again in glory
the prize of eternal life. Amen. ANCIENT PRAYER

FOR THE LIGHT OF HIS COMING

The people that walked in darkness
have seen a great light;
on those who live in a land of shadows,
a light has dawned.

For a child is born for us,
and a son is given to us,
and dominion rests on his shoulders;
this is the name he will bear:
    Wonderful Counsellor,
    Mighty God,
    Everlasting Father,
    Prince of Peace.

Of his kingdom's growth,
    and of peace,
there will be no end—
from David's throne
and over his kingdom,
which he helps and upholds
with justice and integrity,
from this moment on and forever.   IS 9:2, 6–7

Mercifully listen to our prayers, Lord,
and enlighten the darkness of our minds
by the light of your coming. Amen.
                   GELASIAN SACRAMENTARY

THE "O" ANTIPHONS

Wisdom is quicker than any movement
and is so pure
as to pervade and pierce through all things.
She is the breath of the power of God.
She uses her strength
reaching from one end of the earth
to the other,
and ordering all things for good.   WIS 7:24–25; 8:1

O WISDOM,
that came from the lips of the Most High;
you reach out to the ends of the earth,
putting all things in harmony
by the firmness and gentleness
of your touch.
COME to us now,
and teach us your ways of prudence.   ROMAN BREVIARY

DECEMBER 18TH

On Horeb, the mountain of God,
the Lord appeared
in the form of a flame of fire,
coming from the middle of a bush;
there was the bush burning,
but it was not burnt up.   EX 3:2

On the third day,
at daybreak,
there were peals of thunder
and lightning flashes
and a dense cloud over the mountain.
The mountain, Sinai,
was completely wrapped in smoke,
because the Lord came down to it
in the form of fire.   EX 19:16, 18

O ADONAI,
Israel's guide,
you appeared to Moses in a burning bush
and again when you gave him your commands
on Sinai.
Stretch out your hand once again, and
COME to save us.

45

A shoot shall sprout
from the stock of Jesse;
a bud shall blossom
from his roots:
the Spirit of the Lord
shall rest on him—
    a spirit of wisdom
        and understanding,
    a spirit of counsel
        and might,
    a spirit of knowledge
        and fear of the Lord,
and his delight shall be
        the fear of the Lord.

He shall not judge by appearances,
nor make decisions based on hearsay,
but shall judge the poor with justice,
and decide for the needy with uprightness.   IS 11:1-4

O ROOT OF JESSE,
set up as an ensign for your people,
kings are silent in your presence,
and the nations sue for peace;
COME to us now,
and deliver us.
Delay no longer.

I will place
the key to the House of David
upon his shoulder;
when he opens,
no one will shut,
when he shuts,
no one opens.
I will drive him like a peg
into a firm spot,
to be a throne of glory
for his father's house.   IS 22:22-23

O KEY OF DAVID'S CITY,
sceptre of Israel's realm;
who shall ever lock again
what you have unlocked?
or unlock
what you have locked?
COME
and set free your captive people
from their place of imprisonment,
where they sit in darkness
and under the shadow of death.

47

DECEMBER 21ST

I see him,
but not at the present time;
I behold him,
but not yet at hand.
A star shall rise
    out of Jacob,
and a staff shall rise
    out of Israel.   NUM 24:17

O RISING STAR,
brightness of unending light,
and Sun of Justice;
COME
and enlighten those
that sit in darkness,
under the shadow of death.

Draw near to him,
the living stone,
rejected by men,
but chosen by God,
and precious to him.
Become living stones. . . .
Scripture says,
"See how I lay in Sion
a precious corner-stone
chosen by me," and
"he who believes in it
shall not be disappointed."   1 PET 2:4–6

O KING OF THE NATIONS,
object of their yearning,
Corner-stone
that binds the nations together,
COME
and save man,
whom you formed from clay.

The Lord himself
will give you a sign:
a maiden will be with child,
and bear a son,
and will call him "Emmanuel."
He will feed on milk and honey
until he is of the age
to distinguish good from evil.   IS 7:14–16a

O EMMANUEL,
our King and Giver of laws,
Expectation of the nations,
and their Salvation;
COME to save us,
Lord our God.

THE APPEARING, IN GLORY

Your grace, *Lord* God, has been revealed
for the salvation of all men,
and teaches us to renounce
    godlessness and worldly desires,
and to live self-restrained,
    godlike,
    and upright lives
    in this world,
as we await the blessed fulfillment
    of our hope,
the appearing in glory
of our Great God and Savior, Jesus Christ,
who gave himself for us
to redeem us from all sinfulness
and to purify us for himself,
    as a people of his very own,
intent on nothing but good.   TIT 2:11–14

THE CHRISTMAS MARTYROLOGY

In the fullness of time
God sent his only Son,
born of a woman,
born a subject to the Law,
that he might redeem us
    as subjects to the Law,
and gave us the grace
of sons by adoption.   GAL 4:4–5

51

Many ages after the making of the world
when God, in the beginning,
formed the heavens and the earth;
long after the Flood;
some two thousand years
after Abraham's birth;
fifteen centuries after Moses
and the passing over of Israel
out of Egypt;
a thousand years
after David's anointing as king;
in the sixty-fifth week
as Daniel's prophecy takes note;
in the one hundred and ninety-fourth Olympiad,
the seven hundred and forty-second year
from the founding of the City of Rome;
the forty-second year of Octavian Augustus' rule;
in the sixth age of the world,
    all the earth being at PEACE,

JESUS CHRIST
Eternal God,
Son of the Deathless Father,
willing to hallow the world by his coming in mercy,
having been conceived by the Holy Spirit,
and nine months after his conception,
WAS BORN OF THE VIRGIN MARY
IN BETHLEHEM OF JUDA,
GOD MADE MAN.
The Birthday of our Lord Jesus Christ in the flesh.

ROMAN MARTYROLOGY

AN ANTHEM AT CHRISTMAS

Shout for joy, you heavens,
for the Lord has been at work!
Shout aloud, you earth below;
shout aloud, you tall mountains,
    you, forest, and all your trees!
For the Lord has redeemed Jacob,
and shown his glory in Israel.   IS 44:23

THE NEW YEAR

Lord, you have been our refuge age after age.
Before the mountains were born,
before the earth or world came to be,
    you are God from endless ages,
    and for ever.
To you, a thousand years
    are like a single day,
a yesterday now past,
a nighttime hour now over.   PS 90:1-2, 4

God, you are ever the same,
    your years do not fail,
grant that we may so pass this year
    in loving, acceptable service to you,
that lacking nothing of what we need
    for our support,
we may live in perfect submission
    to your commands.   ANCIENT SPANISH LITURGY

EPIPHANY

The sight of the star filled them with joy,
and going into the house
they found the child with Mary, his mother,
and falling to their knees,
they paid him homage.
Then, opening their treasures,
they offered him gifts of gold,
  frankincense, and myrrh.   MT 2:11–12

Almighty, deathless God,
you made known the incarnation of your Word
by the witness of a blazing star,
at sight of which
  the Magi worshiped your majesty,
  and offered gifts;
grant that the star of your justice
may shine forever in our souls,
and that we may find our treasure
in offering you praise.   ANCIENT SPANISH LITURGY

LENTEN PRAYER FOR PARDON

Spare your people, Lord,
do not make your heritage a reproach,
a byword among the nations.
Why should it be said among the peoples,
"Where is their God?"   JOEL 2:17

"HEAR US, LORD . . ."

BAR 3:2

Refrain: Hear us, Lord, and show us mercy,
for we have sinned against you.

King, highly exalted,
all the world's Redeemer,
to you your children
lift their eyes with weeping;
Christ, we implore you,
hear our supplications.   *Refrain*

Right Hand of the Godhead,
Chief Stone at the corner,
Path of salvation,
Gate to heaven's kingdom,
cleanse your people,
bearing stains of sinfulness.   *Refrain*

Begging your eternal majesty,
we make this lamentation
within your holy hearing;
graciously forgive our sins.   *Refrain*

We humbly confess to you,
we who have sinned against you,
all our sins hidden now no longer;
may your redeeming mercy
grant us full pardon.   *Refrain*

Led away captive,
guiltless, unresisting,
charged by false witness,
unto a death for us sinners,
Christ, please protect us
whom your Blood has purchased.   *Refrain*

HYMN OF ROMAN LITURGY

FOR GOD'S MERCY ON HIS CREATION

If I enjoy any favor with you,
then let me speak.
If the farmer's seed does not come up
     because it has not received the seasonal rain,
or because it has been ruined by too much rain,
it perishes.

But man, formed by your hands,
is called your "image,"
for he is made like you,
and for his sake
you have formed all things.

Have you made him like the farmer's seed?
No, Lord, who are over us!
But spare your people,
     pity your inheritance,
for you have mercy on your own creation.   AP 2 ESD 8:42-45

PASSIONTIDE

Far be it from me
to boast in anything,
except in the cross of our Lord Jesus Christ,
through whom the world is crucified to me,
and I to the world.

Circumcision counts for nothing,
as does uncircumcision;
what does count is the new creation!
Peace and mercy upon all those
who live according to this rule!
Peace upon the Israel of God!   GAL 6:14–16

TO THE EXALTED NAME OF CHRIST

Lord, grant us to
have the same attitude as Christ Jesus:
His was the nature of God,
yet he did not esteem equality with God
a thing to be clung to,
but emptied himself,
taking on the nature of a slave,
being born as men are;
and being like other men,
he humbled himself even more,
accepting even death—
        the death on a cross.

Therefore God raised him to greatness,
and gave him the NAME
which is above all other names,
so that, at the name of JESUS,
every creature,
> in heaven,
> on earth,
> or in the world beneath,
should bend the knee,
and every tongue tell out
"Jesus Christ is Lord,"
to the glory of God the Father.   PHIL 2:5-11

Jesus, for your name's sake,
do that which your name proclaims.
Jesus, pardon the pride that pained you,
and look upon the unhappy one
> that calls on your tender name;
Name of comfort,
Name of delight, and to sinners,
Name of blessed hope.
For what does your name mean, Jesus,
> but "Savior?"
Therefore, for your name's sake,
be to me, Jesus,
a Merciful Savior.   ST. AUGUSTINE

FROM THE PSALTER

My God, my God, why have you deserted me,
    dismissing my plea, the words I groan?
My God, I call out by day, and you never answer,
    by night, and I cannot rest,
while you are seated on your throne,
    the Holy One, the Glory of Israel.
In you our fathers put their trust,
    they trusted, and you rescued them;
To you they cried, and they were saved,
    they never trusted you in vain.

But here am I, more a worm than a man,
    the scorn of men, the people's joke!
All who see me make fun of me,
    they gape at me, throw back their heads!
"He lived for the Lord, let him save him!
    Let him rescue him, if he cares for him!"

Yet you drew me out of the womb,
    entrusting me to my mother's breasts;
you placed me on your lap from birth,
    and have been my God from my mother's womb.
Do not stand aside, for danger is near,
    and I have no one to give me help!

A herd of bulls surrounds me,
    wild Bashan bulls close in on me;
Their jaws are open to devour me,
    like roaring, tearing lions.

I am like water, draining away,
    and all my bones are racked;
My heart is like wax,
    melting away within me.
My mouth is drier than a potsherd,
    my tongue sticks to my jaws.

A pack of dogs surrounds me,
    evildoers close in on me;
they pierce my hands and my feet,
    I can count all my bones.
They glare, they stare at me,
    dividing my garments among them,
    casting lots for my cloak.

Do not stand aside, Lord;
    my Strength, hurry to my help.
Rescue my neck from the sword,
    my head from the blade of the axe.
Save me from the lion's mouth,
    my soul from the horns of wild oxen.

Then I shall proclaim your name to my brothers,
    and praise you in their assembly.   PS 22:1–23

PALM SUNDAY

The crowds who had come for the festival
heard that Jesus was on his way to Jerusalem.
They took palm-branches
and went out to meet him, shouting,
"Hosanna!
A blessing on Israel's King,
who comes in the name of the Lord!"   JN 12:12-13

Lord, our Good Redeemer,
who drew near your Passion in meekness,
    on a road all strewn with branches,
    amid waving of triumphal palms,
    and with songs of praise
    sounding in your ears,
we ask your divine majesty
to accept our tribute of praise.

Grant that we too may put forth green leaves,
    and bear good fruit,
so when next you return
we may be found worthy
    to give you joyful welcome,
bearing the palms of victory,
Savior of the world.   ANCIENT SPANISH LITURGY

IN HONOR OF THE HOLY CROSS

One prepares to sail,
and is about to cross raging seas.
Desire for gain produced the vessel,
the shipwright's wisdom built it;
but it is your providence, Father,
that steers its course;
you gave it a path through the oceans,
and a safe way over the waves,
showing that you can save from every danger,
so that, should any man lack the skill,
he may still put out to sea.

It is not your will
that the works of your Wisdom
should be without effect,
and so men trust their lives
to the smallest piece of wood,
and crossing the high seas on a raft,
they can come safely to port.

Even in the beginning,
when proud giants were perishing,
the hope of the world
        found refuge on a raft,
and guided by your hand,
left the world a future to the race of men.

BLESSED IS THE WOOD
BY WHICH RIGHTEOUSNESS COMES.   WIS 14:1-7

EASTER

Christ, having been raised from the dead,
will never die again.
Death no longer has any power over him.
When he died,
he died once and for all, to sin,
and the life he lives now,
he lives with God.   ROM 6:9-10

Christ,
who, being raised from the dead
    will die no more,
grant that sin,
    which is death,
will no longer have mastery over us,
and that we,
    who with ready faith
    proclaim the mystery
    of your Resurrection,
may be delivered from death's mortal sway.
SOURCE UNKNOWN;
ANCIENT PRAYER

FROM THE PSALTER

Sing to the Lord a new song,
    for he has done wondrous deeds;
His own right hand, his holy arm,
    gives him the power to save.

The Lord has made his salvation known,
     showed his righteousness to the nations,
Mindful of his love and faithfulness
     toward the house of Israel.
All the ends of the earth have seen
     the saving power of our God.
Sing to the Lord, all the earth,
     break into song, sing praise!
Sing to the Lord, praises with the harp,
     with harp and every melody;
With trumpets and the sound of the horn,
     sing to the Lord as King!   PS 98:1-6

Give thanks to the Lord, for he is good,
     his love is everlasting!
Let the house of Israel say,
     "His love is everlasting!"
Let the house of Aaron say,
     "His love is everlasting!"
Let all who fear the Lord say,
     "His love is everlasting!"
Shouts of joy and salvation,
     in the tents of the upright:
"The right hand of the Lord has struck with power,
the right hand of the Lord is winning,
the right hand of the Lord strikes with power."
I shall not die, but live,
     and make known the works of the Lord!
Though the Lord indeed chastised me,
     he never gave me over to death.
This is the day the Lord has made;
     let us be glad, and take joy in it.   PS 117:1-4, 15-18, 24

ASCENSION DAY

All you peoples, clap your hands,
    shout to God with cries of joy!
For the Lord Most High inspires awe,
    the Great King over all the world.

He brings peoples under our sway,
    nations under our feet;
He chooses our heritage for us—
    the pride of Jacob, whom he loved.

God arises amid shouts of joy,
    the Lord amid trumpet-blasts.
Sound praises to our God, sound praises!
Sound praises to our King, sound praises!

God is King of the whole world,
    sound the hymns of praise!
God is King of the nations,
    he governs from his holy throne.
The nations' leaders gather
    under the people of Abraham's God;
Every power in the world belongs to God!
    He reigns supreme!   PS 47

PENTECOST

When the day of Pentecost came round,
they were all together in one room,
when suddenly there came a sound—
    like a powerful wind from heaven—
whose noise filled the whole house
    in which they were sitting;
on each of them there appeared
what seemed like tongues of fire,
that separated, and rested
      on the heads of each.
They were all filled with the Holy Spirit
and began to speak foreign languages
as the Spirit gave them the gift of speech.
Now there were devout men
living in Jerusalem,
from every nation under heaven,
and at this sound they gathered,
each one amazed at hearing these men
    speaking in his own language.   ACTS 2:1–5

Almighty, deathless God,
whose will it was
that the mystery of Easter
should be fulfilled in that of Pentecost,
grant through heaven's grace
that the nations,
    torn asunder by difference,
may be made one
in the avowal of your holy name.   SOURCE UNKNOWN

66

FEAST OF THE TRANSFIGURATION

Jesus took Peter, James and John,
and went up the mountain to pray.
As he prayed,
the look on his face was changed,
and his clothes became brilliant—
    like lightning.

Suddenly, two men were there,
    talking with him;
    they were Moses and Elijah,
    appearing in glory,
and they were speaking about his pass-over,
which he was to accomplish in Jerusalem.   LK 9:28-31

Glory to you, spiritual Light,
who, being transfigured on the mountain,
showed the power of your Godhead.

We laud and praise you,
    Mary, virgin-mother,
    who bore in your womb,
knowing all that would come to pass,
    the Light of God become flesh.

One flash of light frightened the Apostles,
but you, Mary, virgin-mother,
held the burning flame of Godhead
    in all its fullness.

A bright, cloud enfolded the Apostles,
but you, holy Mother of God,
were overshadowed by the Holy Spirit,
    by the power of the Most High God.
Christ our God, grant that with Peter,
    and the sons of Zebedee,
we may gaze upon your grandeur.
Lead us onward from the earthly mountain
to your spiritual home,
far above the heavens.

This day
God's mountains thrill with joy,
meeting their Maker,
while prophets and apostles share the joy
    of the eternal hills.

This day
the heavenly Sion,
    Bride of the immortal King,
is filled with joy to see her Bridegroom
splendid, with the Father's glory.

This day
the branch from Jesse's stock
flowers on Mount Thabor.

This day
the disciples breathe
the heady perfume of his immortality.

ARMENIAN OFFICE HYMN

FEAST OF ALL SAINTS

We are no longer strangers,
or foreigners;
we are citizens,
like the saints,
and members of God's household.

We help to form a building
that has apostles and prophets
    for foundation,
and Christ Jesus himself
    as corner-stone.   EPH 2:19-20

Prophets,
Apostles,
Martyrs,
Holy fathers,
pray ceaselessly to him
from whom you received your crown;
may we who keep your worshipful feast,
    in faith and love,
be delivered from all our foes
whether seen or unseen.   EASTERN LITURGIES

THE END OF TIME

May the Lord make *our* love increase,
overflowing towards one another,
    and towards all men,
that he may make our hearts
    firm,
    faultless,
    and holy,
before our God and Father
when the Lord Jesus comes,
    with all his holy ones.

May the God of peace
make *us* thoroughly holy,
and faultless,
and sound in soul and body,
at the coming of our Lord Jesus Christ.   I THESS 3:12–13
                                                              5:23

THE COMING OF THE SON OF MAN

Hosanna!
Blessings on him
who comes in the name of the Lord!

Blessed is the kingdom
    of our father David,
which is coming!
Hosanna
in the highest heavens!   MK 11:9–10

3. God

TO KNOW THE LORD

Come,
let us return to the Lord:
he will heal us,
he will bind our wounds.

After two days
    he will revive us,
on the third day,
    he will raise us up,
and we will live in his presence.

Let us know,
let us press on to know,
    the Lord;
his coming to us is as certain as the dawn,
he will come to us like the showers,
like the spring rains
that sprinkle the earth.   HOS 6:1-3

BLESSED BE GOD

Blessed be God!   PS 68:35
Blessed be the Lord, Israel's God,
who made heaven and earth.   2 CHRON 2:12

Blessed be the Lord,
the God of our fathers.   EZRA 7:27

Blessed be my Rock,
and exalted be my God,
the rock of my salvation.   2 SAM 22:47

Blessed be the Lord, Israel's God,
who fulfilled with his hand
what his mouth had promised.   I KINGS 8:15

Blessed be the Lord,
for he heard the voice of my prayer.   PS 28:6

Blessed be God,
for he has wondrously shown me
his unfailing love.   PS 31:21

Blessed be God,
who alone does these wonderful things!
Blessed be his glorious name forever!   PS 72:18–19

Blessed be the Lord, Israel's God,
from everlasting to everlasting!
And let all people say, "Amen!"   PS 106:48

THE EVERLASTING GOD

The Lord is an everlasting God,
he marked out the boundaries of earth.

He does not grow tired or weary,
his understanding lies beyond our ken.

He gives strength to the wearied,
gives support to the defenseless.

Young men may grow tired or weary,
youths may stumble,
but those who trust in the Lord
    renew their strength,
they put on wings,
    like eagles.

They run, and do not get tired,
they walk, and never flag.   IS 40:28–31

THE HOLINESS OF GOD

You are the Holy One;
you dwell within the holy place,
the praise of Israel.   PS 22:3

Holy! Holy! Holy
is the Lord of hosts!
His glory fills the whole world!   IS 6:3

Holy! Holy! Holy
is the Lord God,
the almighty!
He was,
and is,
and is to come!

You are our Lord and God,
and worthy to receive
    glory,
     honor, and
      power,
for you made all things,
and only by your will
were they made,
and continue to be.   REV 4:4, 11

THE SOVEREIGNTY OF GOD

I now praise the Most High,
and bless and honor him
who lives for ever!

For his dominion
is an everlasting dominion,
and his kingdom
lasts from age to age.   DAN 4:34–35

THE WORKINGS OF GOD

May the grace
    of the Lord Jesus Christ,
and the love
    of God,
and the fellowship
    of the Holy Spirit,
be with *us* all. Amen.   2 COR 13:14

GOD, FAITHFUL IN ALL HIS PROMISES

Blessed be the Lord,
who has granted rest
to his people, Israel,
keeping all his promises;
of all the promises of good he made,
    through Moses his servant,
not even one has failed.
May the Lord our God be with us,
as he was with our fathers.
May he never abandon us,
     nor cast us off.
May he turn our hearts toward him
that we may follow all his ways,
and keep the
     commands,
     laws,
     and precepts
that he gave to our fathers.
May these words of mine,
my prayer before the Lord,
come into the Lord's presence
day and night,
that he may uphold his servant's cause,
and the cause of his people;
may all the peoples of the earth
come to know
that the Lord is indeed God,
and that there is no other. Amen.   I KINGS 8:56–6

THE NAMES OF GOD

I know, Lord,
that the Most High is called "Merciful,"
because he has mercy
on those not yet born into the world;
                    and "Gracious,"
because he is gracious
to those who turn to his Law, repenting;
                    and "Patient,"
because he shows patience
to those who have sinned;
                    and "Bountiful,"
for he would rather give
than take away;
                    and "Compassionate,"
because he makes his compassion abound
more and more,
        to those now alive,
        to those who are gone, and
        to those yet to be born,
for if it did not abound,
the world, and all who dwell on it,
would have no life;
                    and "Giver,"
for if he did not give, out of goodness,
so that sinners might be free from sin,
not one ten-thousandth of mankind
would have life;

and "Judge,"
for if he did not forgive those
who were fashioned by his word,
blotting out their countless wrongs,
there would probably be only a few left
out of the countless numbers of men.   AP 2 ESD 7:62–70

YOU ARE MY GOD

You are my God   PS 143:10
the everlasting God
the Creator of the ends of the earth,   IS 40:28
the God of the whole world;   IS 54:5
the living God,   MT 26:63
the God of our fathers;   ACTS 5:30
the God of Truth,   IS 65:16
            of patience,   ROM 15:5
            of hope,   ROM 15:13
the God of all grace,   I PET 5:10
the God of my salvation,   HAB 3:18
the God of love and peace;   2 COR 13:11
the God of my great joy,   PS 43:4
my salvation and my glory,
the rock of my strength,   PS 62:7
the one God,
and Father of us all.   EPH 4:6

THE LORD IS MY DELIVERER

The LORD is
    my Rock,
    my Fortress,
    and my Deliverer,   PS 18:2
who delivered his people
    from the power of Egypt,   EX 18:11
who delivered David his servant,   PS 144:10
who delivered Daniel from the power of the lions,   DAN 6:27
who delivers the defenseless
    from anyone too strong for him;   PS 35:10
the LORD will deliver me
    from every evil,
and save me
    for his heavenly kingdom.   2 TIM 4:18

The Father

GOD, OUR FATHER

For us there is one God,
the FATHER
from whom all things come,
and for whom we exist;   I COR 8:6
do not let your compassion go unmoved,
for you are our Father,   IS 63:16
the Father of mercies
and the God of all comfort,   2 COR 1:3
the Father of lights,
with whom there is no alteration,
not even a shadow of change,   JAS 1:17
the God and Father
of our Lord Jesus Christ;   EPH 1:3
we are the clay,
you, the Potter;
we are all the work of your hands.
You, Lord, are our Father,
Our Redeemer,
this is your eternal name.   IS 63:16

GOD, OUR SAVIOR AND KING

Let all men be struck with awe
in the presence of the God of Daniel!
    He is the living God,
    he lives for ever!

His sovereignty resists overthrow,
and his kingship can never end.
He it is
who saves,
and sets free,
who works signs
and wonders,
throughout earth and heaven.
He has snatched Daniel
from the power of the lions.   <small>DAN 6:26–28</small>

GOD THE ALMIGHTY

There is no other God
whose care is for all men,
that you need ever show
that you have not judged justly;
nor can any king,
     any ruler,
confront you
about those you have corrected.
You are righteous,
you rule with integrity,
deeming it foreign to your power
to condemn a man
undeserving of punishment.
Your strength
is the source of all justice,
and your sovereignty over all
causes you to pardon all.

You show your strength
when men doubt
the fullness of your power,
and you rebuke the insolence
of those who are aware of it.
You are sovereign in strength,
    mild in judging;
you govern us with forbearance,
for you have power to act
whenever you choose.   WIS 12:13–18

THE SPLENDOR OF GOD

How rich are *your* depths, God,
how deep *your* wealth,
    and wisdom,
    and knowledge!
How unsearchable *your* judgments,
how untraceable *your* ways!
For "Who has known the Lord's mind,
    or been his counsellor?"
or "Who has given him a gift
    that he must be repaid?"
For from *you*
    through *you*
    and to *you*
all things belong!
To *you* be the honor
    and the glory
for ever! Amen.   ROM 11:33–36

OUR REDEEMER FOREVER

Look down from heaven,
look down from your dwelling-place,
    holy and glorious.

Where are your zealous care?
    Your might?
    Your surge of pity?
    Your compassion?

Lord,
do not hold them back,
for you are our Father.
Were Abraham to ignore us,
were Israel to ignore us,
you, Lord, are still our Father,
bearing the name
"Our Redeemer Forever."

Yes, Lord,
you are our Father;
we the clay,
you the potter,
we are, all of us,
the work of your hands.
Consider this:
we are all your people.

IS 63:15–16
64:8–9

THE GOD IN WHOM WE LIVE

The God who made the world,
    and everything in it,
being Lord of earth and heaven,
does not live in shrines
    built by men,
nor is he served by human hands
as though he needed anything,
since he himself gives to all men
    life,
    breath, and
    everything.

You have made from one man
    every nation of men
to live on the face of the earth,
    setting seasons to their growth
    laying boundaries to their lands,
that they might search for *you*,
hoping they might grope for *you*
and find *you*.
Yet *you* are not far
    from each of us,
and in *you*
    we live,
    and move,
    and are.   ACTS 17:24–28

The Son

CHRIST, THE ETERNAL PRIEST

God, our Father,
since we have a great high priest
    who passed through the heavens,
in Jesus Christ, the Son of God,
let us hold fast
to the faith we profess.
For we do not have a high priest
    unable to feel for us
    in our weakness,
but one who,
    because of his likeness to us,
endured every temptation we have,
    only without sinning.
Let us draw near with confidence
to *your* throne of grace,
that we may have mercy
    and receive grace
for every time of need. Amen.   HEB 4:14–16

JESUS, THE CHRIST

Jesus *is* the Christ,
    risen from the dead,
    sprung from David's lineage,
    preached by the Gospel:

if we have died with him,
    we shall live with him;
if we hold firm,
    we shall reign with him;
if we deny him,
    he shall deny us;
but
if we are faithless,
    he shall remain faithful,
for he cannot deny himself.   2 TIM 2:8, 11–13

JESUS, GOD'S HOLY ONE

Lord,
to whom shall we go?
Your words are eternal life.
We have believed,
and therefore know,
that you
are the Holy One of God!
I believe that you
are the Messiah,
    the Son of God,
    the One who was to come
into the world.   JN 6:68–69;
    11:27

JESUS, THE ONE SENT BY GOD

Father, the hour has come!
Glorify your Son,
   that your Son
may glorify you.
You have given him
dominion over all mankind,
to give eternal life
to all whom you have given him.
Eternal life is this:
to know you,
   the only true God,
and Jesus Christ,
   whom you have sent.   JN 17:1–3

CHRIST, THE WAY, TRUTH, AND LIFE

I am the Way,
   the Truth,
   and the Life.
No one comes to the Father
except by me.
If you know me,
   you know my Father as well;
from this moment
you know
and have seen him.   JN 14:6–7

Lord Jesus, the Way,
    the Truth,
    and the Life,
we pray
not to let us stray from you,
    the Way,
nor to distrust you,
    the Truth,
nor to rest in anyone but you,
    the Life.
By the Holy Spirit
teach us what to do,
    what to believe,
    and wherein to take our rest.
For your own name's sake
we ask this.   ERASMUS

A LITANY TO CHRIST

I AM the bread of life,
I AM the bread
that came down from heaven.   JN 6:35, 41
Lord, always give us this bread!   JN 6:34
I AM the door.
If anyone enters by me
he will be saved.   JN 10:9
Lord, Lord, open to us!   MT 25:11

I AM the light to the world.
Whoever follows me
will have the light of life. JN 8:12
Send us your truth and your light! PS 43:3
I AM the good shepherd.
The good shepherd lays down his life
for his flock. JN 10:11
I pray there will be one flock, one shepherd! JN 10:16
I AM the resurrection and the life.
Whoever lives and believes in me
shall never die. JN 11:25
For me to live is Christ, to die is gain! PHIL 1:21
I AM the way, the truth and the life.
No one comes to the Father
except by me. JN 14:6
Show me your ways, Lord, teach me your paths! PS 25:4
I AM he who searches mind and heart,
and will give to each of you
as your works deserve. REV 2:23
Search me, God, and know my heart! PS 139:23
I AM the root
and offspring of David,
the bright morning star. REV 22:16
Have mercy on me, Son of David! MT 15:22
I AM Alpha and Omega,
the first and the last,
the beginning and the end. REV 22:13
Teach us that the first shall be last,
the last first! MT 19:30

CHRIST, THE LAMB OF GOD

You are worthy to take the scroll
    and to break its seal,
for you were sacrificed,
and with your blood
you ransomed men for God
    out of every tribe,
        and tongue,
        and nation,
        and people,
and made of them a kingdom,
and they shall be priests
    to serve our God
    and reign upon earth.

Worthy is the Lamb
    that was slain
to receive power and strength,
        wealth and wisdom,
        honor and glory
        and blessing.
To him who sits upon the throne
and to the Lamb
be honor and blessing,
    glory and strength,
for ever and ever, Amen.　　REV 5:9–10, 12–13

IN PRAISE OF CHRIST OUR GOD

May grace and peace be *ours*
from him who was
    and is
    and is to come;
from the seven spirits
    before his throne;
from Jesus Christ,
    the faithful witness,
    first-born from the dead,
    ruler over earth's rulers.

To him who loves us,
    who freed us from our sins
    by his blood,
making of us a kingdom of priests
    to his God and Father,
to him be glory,
    and honor
for ever and ever. Amen.

See, he is coming on the clouds,
and every eye shall see him,
even those who pierced him. Amen!   REV 1:4-7

MORE THAN CONQUERERS

Who can separate us
from Christ's love?
Can worry?
    Persecution?
    Hunger?
    Nakedness?
    Danger?
    Weapons?
By no means!

In all these things
we are more than conquerers
through him who loved us.
    I am sure
that neither death,
    nor life,
    nor angels,
    nor principalities,
    nor things present,
    nor things to come,
    nor powers,
    nor height,
    nor depth,
    nor anything else
    in all creation,
can separate us
from the love of God
in Christ Jesus our Lord!   ROM 8:35-39

The Holy Spirit

THE SPIRIT OF GOD

Holy Spirit,
you help *us* in our weakness,
for we do not know
how to pray properly;
you intercede for us
with a plea too deep for words,
and God, who searches deep things,
knows what is in *your* mind.

You pray
    for God's own people
    in God's own way.
We know that in everything
you work for good
with those who love God,
    who have been called
according to his purpose.

Those who are his he knew beforehand;
these he ordained to be formed
    in the likeness of his Son,
that he might be "first"
among many brothers.
These "fore-ordained" he has called,
these "called" he has justified,
these "justified" he raised to glory.   ROM 8:26–34

FOR THE GIFTS OF THE SPIRIT

Suffering brings patience,
patience brings perseverance,
and perseverance brings hope,
a hope that does not disappoint,
for the love of God
has been poured into our hearts,
by the Holy Spirit
who was given to us.   ROM 5:4-5

Almighty God,
to whom all hearts are open,
    all desires known,
from whom no secrets are hidden,
cleanse the thoughts of our hearts
by the inpouring of the Holy Spirit,
that we may love you perfectly,
and worthily praise your holy Name.
        Amen.   GELASIAN SACRAMENTARY

GIFT OF THE SPIRIT

Blessed be the name of God,
    for ever and ever,
for wisdom and might are his.

He causes the changes of times
    and seasons,
makes kings, and unmakes kings.

He gives WISDOM to the wise,
KNOWLEDGE to those who have UNDERSTANDING;
He reveals things deep and hidden,
and knows what lies in darkness,
for with him is light.

To you, God of my fathers,
I give thanks and praise,
for you have given me wisdom
    and STRENGTH,
and have made known to me
what we have asked of you. Amen.   DAN 2:20–23

4. The Church

GOD'S HOUSEHOLD

We are God's household,
    the Church of the living God,
    the pillar and bulwark of truth.
Deep indeed is the mystery of our religion,
Jesus Christ:
    he was made manifest in the flesh,
    attested to by the Spirit,
    seen by angels;
    proclaimed to the nations,
    believed in by the world,
    taken into glory.   I TIM 3:14–16

FOR GOD'S BLESSING ON HIS PEOPLE

May the Lord bless and keep *us*;
May the Lord let his face shine on *us*
    and be gracious to *us*;
May the Lord reveal his face to *us*,
    and bring *us* peace!   NUM 6:24–26

We have come to Mount Sion,
to the city of the living God,
    the heavenly Jerusalem,
to countless angels,
    in a festive gathering,
to the assembly of the first-born,
    who are enrolled in heaven,
to a Judge,
    who is the God of all,
to the spirits of just men,
    who are made perfect,
to Jesus,
    the mediator of a new covenant.   HEB 12:22-24
I believe
    Christ loved the Church,
    and gave himself up for her,
    that he might make her holy,
    that the Church might be presented
    in splendor before him;   EPH 5:25-27
I believe
    Christ is the head of the Church,
    and is himself its Savior; and   EPH 5:23
I complete what is lacking
    in Christ's sufferings,
for the sake of his body, the Church   COL 1:24
    the Church of the Lord,
    which he obtained by his own blood,   ACTS 20:28
    the Church of the living God   I TIM 3:15
to whom be glory in the Church
    and in Christ Jesus,
through all ages, for ever and ever. Amen.   EPH 3:21

THE BODY OF CHRIST

We will always thank *you*, God,
the Father of our Lord Jesus Christ!
He is the image of the unseen God,
born before all creation;
in him were made all things,
    in heaven and on earth,
    seen and unseen—
    whether thrones or dominions,
    principalities or powers—
all things were made
    through him
    and for him.
He exists before all things,
and he holds all things together.
He is the head of his body,
    the Church.
He is its beginning,
the first to come back from death,
that he might be first in all things.
For in him the completeness of God,
by *your* own choice,
was embodied,
to reconcile to *yourself*, through him,
all things,
whether on earth or in heaven,
making peace
by the blood he shed on the cross.   <small>COL 1:3, 15–20</small>

PRAYER OF THE BODY OF CHRIST

May the God
    of our Lord Jesus Christ,
    the Father of glory,
give *us* a spirit of wisdom
to perceive what has been revealed,
to bring *us* to full knowledge about him.
May he enlighten the eyes of *our* mind,
that *we* can see the hope
    which he holds out to us;
    the rich glories
    which his saints will inherit; and
    the great power
    which he has worked in us believers,
and which he accomplished in Christ
    when he raised him from the dead,
    when he made him sit at his right hand
in heaven,
far above all rule, and authority,
    all power, and dominion,
far above every name that can be named,
not only in this age,
but in any age to come.
He has put all things under his feet;
he has made him
    head over all things,
    head of the Church, his body,
the fullness of him who fills all things.   EPH 1:17-23

THE CHURCH'S SONG OF DELIVERANCE

I will sing to the Lord,
  glorious and triumphant;
both horse and rider
  he has thrown into the sea.
The Lord is my strength
  my song,
and he is my Savior!
This is my God, I praise him!
My father's God, I extol him!
The Lord is a warrior,
  "Lord" is his name!
Your right hand, Lord,
  is majestic in power.
Among the Gods, Lord,
  who is like you?
    Majestic in holiness!
    Fearful in deeds of glory!
    Worker of wonders!
In your loyal love,
you led the people you redeemed,
and by your power,
guided them to your holy house.   EX 15:1-13

FOR BLESSINGS ON THE CHURCH

A blessing on the one
    who reads this prophecy;
a blessing on the one who hears,
    if what is written is kept.   REV 1:3
A blessing on those
    who die in the Lord;
a blessing indeed,
    for they can rest from their works,
    since their deeds go with them.   REV 14:13
A blessing on one who is watchful,
    keeping his garments,
    that he may not go naked,
    ashamed before all.   REV 16:15
A blessing on those
    who are invited
    to the marriage-feast of the Lamb.   REV 19:9
A blessing, and holiness,
    on those who share
    in the first resurrection;
the second death cannot harm them,
but they shall be priests of God and Christ,
and shall reign with him a thousand years.   REV 20:6
A blessing on the one
    who treasures
    the prophecy of this book.   REV 22:7
A blessing on those
    who have washed their robes,
    that they may have access
    to the Tree of Life,
    and may enter the City by its gates.   REV 22:14

THE CHURCH'S PRAISE OF CHRIST

My soul sings out the Lord's greatness,
my spirit finds joy in my saving God,
for he looked upon his lowly handmaid.

Yes, from this day on,
all ages will call me blessed,
for the Mighty One has done great things for me,
and his name is "Holy."

His mercy is from one age to another
for those who revere him:
he has shown the power of his arm,
he has routed the proud of heart;
he has pulled the mighty from their thrones,
he has raised up the lowly and meek;
he has given the poor their fill of good things,
he has sent the rich away without a thing;
he has come to the aid of his servant Israel,
mindful of his mercy (as he promised our fathers)
to Abraham and his children for ever. LK 1:46-56

Lord, the whole assembly of the Church
sings out your greatness, our Redeemer,
with the words of your blessed mother;
you looked with favor on your lowly handmaid,
    both when the Virgin conceived you,
    and when the Church acknowledged you by faith.

From Mary's womb
you came to redeem the Church;
therefore all ages call her "blessed,"
and in the Church
    all peoples find blessedness.

Lord, receive your people Israel;
remember your merciful promise
    made to our fathers,
and let that promise be fulfilled,
by the redemption of all the world.

Merciful God,
stand by your Church,
and continually purify
    your adopted children
    in her bosom,
who, while enclosed in Mary's womb,
hallowed John in the womb of Elizabeth,
and who lives forever. Amen.   ANCIENT SPANISH LITURGY

WHEN A PASTORAL OFFICE IS VACANT

May the Lord,
 the God of the spirits
 of all mankind,
appoint a leader
over this congregation,
to be at their head
 in all they do,
a man to lead them out
 and bring them in;
that the assembly of the Lord
may not be as sheep
 without a shepherd.   NUM 27:15-17

FOR FORGIVENESS FOR THE CHURCH

Let the power of the Lord
be displayed in all its greatness,
as you have sworn, saying:
 "The Lord is slow to anger,
 and rich in loyal love,
 forgiving faults and wrong-doing. . . ."
Pardon, then,
the sin of this people,
I beg you,
out of the richness
 of your loyal love,
even as you have forgiven them
 from Egypt till now.   NUM 14:17-19

FOR MERCY UPON THE CHURCH

Lord God,
do not destroy your people,
    your heritage,
whom in your greatness
you have redeemed,
whom you brought out of Egypt,
    with a mighty hand.

Remember your servants,
    Abraham,
    Isaac,
    and Jacob;
take no heed
of this people's stubbornness,
    their wickedness,
    or their sin.

They are your people,
    and your heritage,
whom you delivered
    by your great power
    and your outstretched arm.   DEUT 9:26-28

FOR THE CHURCH'S WITNESS
TO THE NATIONS

Have mercy on us, Lord,
    God of all,
and look upon us!

Cast the fear of yourself
upon the nations, all of them!

Let them see your might!
As in us you have been proved holy
    before them,
so in them be proven great
    before us;
let them know, as we have known,
that there is no god—only you, Lord.

Show new signs, work new wonders,
win glory for your right arm and hand!

Have mercy, Lord,
upon the people called by your name.
Reward those who wait for you.

Listen, Lord, to your servants' prayers
in accordance with Aaron's blessing
    for your people;
then will all on earth
know that you are the Lord,
    ageless God
    of the ages!   SIR 36:1–17

FOR THE UNITY OF THE CHURCH

Sovereign Lord,
from every forest of the earth
and from all its trees,
     you have chosen for yourself ONE VINE;
from all the lands of the world,
     you have chosen for yourself ONE REGION;
from all the flowers of the land,
     you have chosen for yourself ONE FLOWER;
from all the depths of the ocean,
     you have filled for yourself ONE RIVER;
from all the cities that have been founded,
     you have chosen for yourself SION;
from all the birds that have been fashioned,
     you have chosen for yourself ONE DOVE;
from all the flocks that have been formed,
     you have chosen for yourself ONE SHEEP;
from all the multitudes of peoples,
     you have chosen for yourself ONE PEOPLE;
and to this PEOPLE whom you loved,
     you have given your law, approved by all;
now, Lord, why have you given over the one
                      to the many?

May they all be one.   AP 2 ESD 5:23–28
                             JOHN 17:21

FOR THE UNITY OF THE CHURCHES: CHRIST'S OWN PRAYER

I pray
for all those
who through their words
put their faith in me;
may they all be one,
Father, may they be one in us,
as you are in me,
and I in you.   JN 17:20–21

FOR THE UNITY OF THE CHURCHES

Whatever was written long ago
was written to teach us
    that with firmness,
    and the encouragement
    which Scripture affords,
we might have hope.

May the God of all firmness
    and encouragement
grant *us* to live
in such harmony with one another
    after the example of Jesus Christ,
that *we* may together
    WITH ONE VOICE
praise the God and Father
of our Lord Jesus Christ.

May the God of all hope
fill us with such joy
    and peace,
through our faith in him,
that, by the Holy Spirit's power,
we may overflow with hope.   ROM 15:4-6,13

FOR THE CHURCH'S WORK
OF SALVATION

I saw the holy city, New Jerusalem,
coming down out of heaven, from God.
I heard a voice saying:
"See, this is God's dwelling place with men.
He will make his home among them;
they shall be his people, and he, their God."
His name is "God-with-them."
Then the One who sat upon the throne said,
"See, I am making all things new!"   REV 21:2-5

God of power unchangeable,
     and light unquenchable,
look favorably upon your whole Church,
that sacred and wonderful mystery;
by the tranquil working of your providence
carry out the work of man's salvation;
let the whole world feel and see
that the things that were cast down
     are being raised up,
the things that had grown old
     are being made new,
and all things are returning to perfection
through him from whom they took beginning,
our Lord, Jesus Christ. Amen.   GELASIAN SACRAMENTARY

THE CHURCH, GLORIOUS
IN HER SAINTS

Let us rejoice and be glad,
and give him glory,
for the marriage of the Lamb has come,
his bride has made herself ready;
"it was granted her to be clothed
     with fine linen,
     bright and pure"—
for the fine linen
is the righteous deeds of the saints.   REV 19:7-9

Wearing the blood of your martyrs,
    like purple and fine linen,
the Church cries to you in their name;
Christ our God,
show your loving-kindness to your people,
give peace to our country,
and your mercy to ourselves. Amen.   eastern rite

The Church's Worship

I WORSHIP—1

I worship the one God of heaven,	JUDITH 5:9
that which we know;	JN 4:22
I worship at the dawning of light,	WIS 16:28
in the morning,	I SAM 1:19
even now;	JUDITH 11:14
falling to the ground	2 KINGS 2:15
towards your holy Temple;	PS 5:8
in the house of the Lord	JER 26:2
at his holy mountain;	PS 98:9
I worship with holy becomingness,	I CHRON 16:29
in spirit and in truth,	JN 4:23
with joy.	WIS 35:20

I WORSHIP—2

I worship God,	REV 22:9
the Father, in spirit and truth,	JN 4:22, 23
the God of our fathers,	ACTS 24:14
who made heaven and earth,	
the sea	
and the fountains of water;	REV 14:7
who is seated upon the throne,	REV 19:4
who lives for ever and ever;	REV 4:10
I worship God, in spirit,	
and glory in Christ Jesus;	PHIL 3:3
I worship towards your holy temple.	I CHRON 5:7

BEFORE WORSHIP

May God be good to *us*,
keeping in mind his covenant
    with Abraham,
    Isaac,
    and Jacob,
his faithful servants.
May he give *us* all
a heart to worship him,
    and do his will,
with strong heart
and willing spirit.
May he open *our* hearts
    to his Law
    and his precepts,
and bring *us* peace!
May he hear *our* prayers
and be reconciled to *us*,
and not forsake *us* in time of trouble.

2 MAC 1:2–5 (ADAPTED)

FOR THE FULLNESS OF OUR WORSHIP

I beg you, *Heavenly Father*,
grant us to present
    our very selves to you,
    as a living sacrifice
    holy and acceptable,
the worship that spiritual persons
    should offer.

Do not let us be conformed to this world,
  but transformed,
by the renewal of *our* minds.
This is the way to know
  what the will of God is,
  what is good,
  and acceptable,
  and perfect before *you*. Amen.   ROM 12:1–2 (ADAPTED)

PRAYER FOR ACCEPTABLE WORSHIP

Almighty Father,
let us be thankful
for receiving an unshakeable kingdom,
and let us worship *you*, God,
worship that is acceptable,
  with awe and reverence,
for our God is a consuming fire.
Let brotherly love continue.

May we remember to welcome strangers,
for some have thereby welcomed angels
  without knowing it.
May we be mindful of those in prison,
  as though in prison with them,
and those who are ill-treated,
  since *we* too are in the one body.
May marriage be held in honor by all,
and marriages kept undefiled.

May our lives be free from love of money,
and we content with what we have,
for *you have* said,
"I will never fail nor forsake you."

HEB 11:28–13:5 (ADAPTED)

OUR SACRIFICE OF PRAISE

Lord God, Maker of all things,
    awe-inspiring, strong,
    just, merciful,
    the only King,
    the only Kind One,
only you are bountiful,
only you are just,
    all powerful
    and deathless;
you rescue Israel from every evil,
and chose our fathers,
    to hallow them;
accept this sacrifice
on behalf of all your people,
    preserve your heritage,
    and make it holy.
Gather together those who are scattered,
  set free those who are in prison,
  from among the nations,
look upon all who are rejected
    or despised,
and let the nations know
that you are God. Amen.

2 MAC 1:24–27

THE OFFERING OF ONE'S GIFT

I have removed a sacred portion
    out of my home,
and have given it to the Levite,
               the stranger,
               the fatherless,
          and the widow,
just as you commanded me.
In this I have not transgressed your commands,
    nor forgotten any of them.
I have obeyed the voice of the Lord my God,
and have done all that you commanded me.
Look down, then,
from the dwelling-place of your holiness,
and bless your people,
and the soil you have given us.   DEUT 26:13-15

THE LORD'S SUPPER

This "Cup of Blessing" that we bless,
is a sharing in the Blood of Christ,
    and the "bread" that we break
is a sharing in the Body of Christ.
Since there is only the "one bread"
we, though many,
    are one bread,
    one body,
all of us who share
this "only bread."   I COR 10:16-17

BEFORE APPROACHING THE LORD'S TABLE

Just as the human body,
  though made up of many parts,
  is yet one
because all the parts, though many,
  form one body,
so it is with Christ.
In the One Spirit we were all baptized,
and the One Spirit was given
  to us all as drink.   I COR 12:12-13

Let your Spirit cleanse my heart,
I beg you,
lest I unworthily approach
  your heavenly Table,
that feast which the very angels
  hold in awe.
Let me grow into you,
having you diffused
  through every fibre of my being.
Let my spirit wax in strength,
to persevere in the blessed fellowship
  of your Body mystical,
which you will to be one with you
as you are one,
  with the Father
  and the Holy Spirit.
To Whom be praise and thanksgiving
for ever and ever. Amen.   DESIDERIUS ERASMUS

FOR ALL WHO HAVE WORSHIPED

All things come from you;
from your hand
we have given your own to you,
for we are strangers before you,
    only settlers,
as were all our fathers.
I know, my God,
that you judge the heart,
and take delight in integrity;
in the integrity of my heart
I have freely offered all these things,
and with joy I have seen your people here
freely offering their gifts to you.
Lord, God of Abraham,
    Isaac,
    and Jacob,
keep forever such purpose and thoughts
    in the hearts of your people,
and direct their hearts to you. Amen.

I CHRON 29:14–18

Come, bless the Lord,
    all you who serve the Lord,
    standing in the house of the Lord,
    in the courts of the house of our God.
Stretch your hands to the Holy Place,
and bless the Lord each night.
May the Lord bless you, from Sion,
the Maker of heaven and earth.   PS 134

Turning to the Lord our God,
let us earnestly pray to him
    for ourselves,
    and for all his People,
who with us stand
    in the house of the Lord,
that he may deign to guard us
    and protect us
through Jesus Christ our Lord,
    his Son,
who lives and reigns with him
for ever and ever. Amen.   ST. AUGUSTINE

5. *The Christian*

Baptism

CHRIST, LIVING IN ME

I have been crucified
    with Christ;
it is no longer I
    whom am living,
    but Christ,
living in me;
the life I now live
    in this body,
I live by faith,
    by faith in God's Son,
who loved me,
and gave himself for me.   GAL 2:20

THE TREASURE OF GOD'S FAVOR

The same God who said,
"Let light shine
out of darkness,"
has shone within our minds
to spread the light
of the knowledge of God's glory,
        the glory that is seen
        in the face of his Christ.
But we are only earthen vessels
that hold this treasure,
to show that this tremendous power
        comes from God,
        and not from ourselves.   2 COR 4:6-7

Lord,
make us worthy to experience
within our person,
the resurrection for which we hope.
Be a wing to our thoughts,
that we may fly swift
        through the air,
borne, as on wings,
to our true home.
With the grace of BAPTISM
we hide your treasure
within our bodies;
grant us to rejoice
in the increase of this treasure. Amen.   ST. EPHRAIM

BURIAL WITH CHRIST

When we were baptized in Christ Jesus
    we were baptized into his death;
therefore, when we were baptized
we went into the tomb with him,
    joining him in death,
so that,
as Christ was raised from the dead
    by the glory of the Father,
we too might live that new life.
If, together with Christ,
    we have imitated his death,
so too shall we also imitate
    his holy resurrection.   ROM 6:3-5

Lord Christ,
with whom we lay buried in death together,
    so that we might rise again
    by faith in your resurrection,
wash away our sins in your Blood,
and do not cease to purify us
    by your merciful forgiveness
whom you have long since cleansed
in the waters of Baptism. Amen.   ANCIENT PRAYER
                                    SOURCE UNKNOWN

DEATH TO SIN

Heavenly Father,
if we have been joined to Christ
    in a death like his,
we shall certainly be one with him
    in a resurrection like his.
We know that the person we once were
    was crucified with him,
that the sinful self
    might be put to death,
and we might be no longer
    the slaves of sin.

When one dies,
he is free of sin;
we believe
    that if we died with Christ
    we shall live with him,
for we know that Christ,
    being raised from the dead
    can never die again.
Death has no dominion over him any more.
The death he died
    he died to sin,
    once and for all,
but the life he now lives
    he lives with *you*:
Teach us to consider *ourselves*
    as dead to sin,
    but alive to *you*,
in Christ Jesus. Amen.

ROM 6:5-11

124

LIFE IN CHRIST

We may be hard-pressed in every way,
 but not crushed;
or perplexed,
 but not driven to despair;
hunted down,
 but not forsaken;
or struck down,
 but not destroyed.

We are always carrying
 in our bodies
 the death of Jesus,
 that the life of Jesus
may be made known
 in our bodies.

As long as we live
we are always being given up to death
 for the sake of Jesus,
 that the life of Jesus
may be made known
 in our mortal flesh.   2 COR 4:6–11

PUTTING ON CHRIST

Grant us, your chosen ones,
    your beloved ones,
to put on garments
    of kindness,
    compassion,
    lowliness,
    meekness, and
    patience;
to bear with one another;
to forgive one another,
    if there is an argument;
to put on love
    over all these garments,
    for it binds them together
    and completes the garb.

May Christ's peace rule
    from *our* hearts,
for to that peace *we* were called
    in the one body.
Let us be thankful.

May Christ's word dwell in us
    richly;
may we counsel each other
    with all wisdom,
as *we* sing psalms and hymns
    and spiritual songs,
making thankful melody to God
    in our hearts.

Whatever we do, be it word or work,
may we do all
in the name of our Lord, Jesus Christ,
giving thanks to *you*, Father,
through him. Amen. COL 3:12–17

THE ROBE OF SALVATION

As many of *us*
as were baptized in Christ
have put on Christ. GAL 3:27

I take great joy in the Lord,
and my soul takes joy in my God,
for he has clothed me
    with the garment of righteousness,
as a bridegroom is adorned
    with a garland,
as a bride is adorned
    with jewels.

For as the earth brings forth shoots,
and a garden makes its growth spring up,
so will the Lord
    make praise and righteousness
spring up before all the nations. IS 61:10–11

PRAISE TO GOD FOR OUR BAPTISM

Blessed be God
    the Father
    of our Lord Jesus Christ!

By his great mercy
we have been re-born
    into a living hope
through the raising from the dead
    of Jesus Christ,
    and into a heritage
that is undying,
    unfading,
    undefiled,
and kept for *us* in heaven.

By God's power,
through *our* faith,
he will keep *us* safe
until the salvation
    that has been prepared
has been revealed,
    at the end of time.   I PET 1:3–5

Christian Life

FOR CONFIRMATION OF OUR WORDS

The Lord Jesus, after he spoke with them,
was taken up into heaven,
and took his place there
at the right hand of God,
while they (Apostles) went out
preaching everywhere,
the Lord working with them
and confirming their word
by the signs that accompanied it.   MK 16:19–20

May it be, Lord Christ,
that our words,
     which bespeak your glory,
shall be confirmed
     by signs and deeds,
that we may at last be perfect,
you co-operating in all our words
     and works,
for yours is the glory both of words
     and works. Amen.   THEOPHYLACTUS

FOR A CHRISTIAN LIFE OF SERVICE

Thanks be to God, who gives us a share
in the triumph of Christ,
and through us
is spreading the fragrance of Christ everywhere,
the sweet odor of his knowledge.   2 COR 2:14

Teach me to profit
by the suffering that comes across my path.
Let me so use it that it may mellow me,
not harden nor embitter me,
that it may make me patient,
not irritable,
that it may make me broad in my forgiveness,
not narrow, haughty, nor overbearing.
May no one be less good
for having come within my influence;
no one less pure,
          less true,
          less kind,
          less noble
for having been a fellow-traveler
in our journey toward eternal life.
As I go my rounds
from one distraction to another,
let me whisper
from time to time
a word of love to you.
May my life be lived in the supernatural,
full of power for good,
and strong in its purpose of holiness.

Lord Jesus,
help me to spread your fragrance everywhere.
Flood my soul with your Spirit and life;
penetrate and possess my whole being
     so completely
that my life may only be
a radiance of yours.
Shine through me,
and be so in me
that every soul
with whom I come in contact
may feel your presence
within my soul.
Let them look up
and no longer see me,
but only you, Jesus.   JOHN HENRY NEWMAN

THE CHRISTIAN—FOLLOWER OF CHRIST

The Lord has given me
     a disciple's tongue,
that I may know how to reply
     to the weary;
he supplies the words to tell them.
Each morning he wakes me
     to hear,
     to listen
like his disciple.
The Lord has opened my ear.   IS 50:4

FOR A CHRISTIAN LIFE

We ask *you*, God,
that through perfect wisdom
    and spiritual insight,
we may reach full knowledge
    of your will;
to live the kind of life
    pleasing to you, Lord,
    full worthy of *you*,
bearing fruit by every kind of good work,
and growing in the knowledge of God.

May we receive strength,
by *your* own glorious power,
    to never give in,
    but to bear all things in joy,
thanking *you*, Father,
    for making us fit
    to be one with God's people
    and share the Light with them.

By what *you have* done,
you delivered us from the power of darkness,
and settled us in the kingdom of *your* Son,
in whom we have gained our freedom
and the forgiveness of our sins.   col 1:9–14

FOR A DEDICATED CHRISTIAN LIFE

You raise grass for the cattle,
  and plants for man to tend,
that he may bring food out of the earth,
  wine to gladden men's hearts,
  oil to make their faces gleam,
  and bread to make them strong.   PS 104:14-15

Grant to our souls, Lord,
the BREAD of earthly reality
  to nourish them,
the WINE of created beauty
  to intoxicate them, and
the DISCIPLINE of human struggle
  to make them strong.
       PIERRE TEILHARD DE CHARDIN

FOR AN ACTIVE LOVE

Lord, may we
be watchful,
standing firm in *our* faith,
be courageous and strong;
let all that *we* do
be done in love. Amen.   I COR 16:13-14

PRAYER OF HUSBAND OR WIFE

You are blessed, my God,
with every pure and holy blessing;

Let your saints and all creatures
    bless you!

Let your angels and all your chosen people
    bless you,
    for ever!

You are blessed
because you made me glad,
and have treated us
with mercy beyond measure!

You are blessed
because you showed compassion
on two children.

Show *us* mercy, Lord,
and let *us* fulfill *our* lives
    in health,
    in happiness,
    and in love. Amen.

TOB 8:15–17

A MARRIAGE PLEDGE

Wherever you go, I will go;
wherever you live, I will live.

Your people shall be my people,
and your God, my God.

Wherever you die, I will die,
and there will I be buried.

May the Lord do what he wills to me,
and more besides,
if even death should separate me
      from you.   RUTH 1:16–17

FROM THE PSALTER

Happy are those who fear the Lord,
    and follow his ways.

You will eat what your hands have worked for,
    joy and abundance shall be yours.

Your wife shall be like a fruitful vine,
    within the very heart of your home.

Your children shall be round your table
    like shoots round an olive tree.

135

These are the blessings
   that come to the man who fears God.

May the Lord bless you from Sion
   every day of your life!

May you see Jerusalem doing well,
   and live to see your children
   having children!
Peace to Israel.

PS 128

6. *Repentance and Forgiveness*

I REPENT

I repent of the evil I have done	JER 26:3
for my sins,	WIS 12:19
groaning with anguish;	WIS 5:3
I return from wicked ways,	2 KINGS 17:13
as deeply as *I* rebelled;	IS 31:6
with all my heart,	I KINGS 8:48
in peace,	2 CHRON 18:27
striking the breast;	LK 23:48
to the Lord our God,	HOS 6:1
to penance,	2 PET 3:9
to my former state.	EZEK 16:55

A TESTING OF OURSELVES

Examine yourselves	
to make sure you are in the faith,	
and test yourselves.	
Can you acknowledge	
that Jesus Christ is truly within you?	2 COR 13:5

Lord God,
to whom all hearts are open,
    all desires known,
from whom no secrets are hidden,
enlighten our minds
by the pouring of the Holy Spirit;
give us grace
    to know our sins,
    to love you perfectly,
    and to praise you worthily.
Through Christ our Lord. Amen.   RACCOLTA

BEFORE SEARCHING AND
EXAMINING OUR WAYS

The Lord will not cast aside forever,
but though he punishes,
he will have compassion,
out of the abundance of his loyal love;
for he does not afflict
    nor grieve
the sons of men with any joy.

Let us search and examine our ways,
and return to the Lord!
Let us lift up hearts and hands
to God in heaven!
"We have sinned and rebelled,
and you have not yet forgiven!"   LAM 3:31-33, 40-42

AN EXAMEN OF CONSCIENCE

THE COMMANDS OF GOD:
I am the Lord your God:
you shall have no other gods before me.
You shall not take the name of your God to misuse it.
Remember the Sabbath day, and keep it holy.
Honor your father and mother.
You shall not kill.
You shall not commit adultery.
You shall not steal.
You shall not bear false witness against your neighbor.
You shall not covet your neighbor's house.
You shall not covet your neighbor's wife,
     nor anything that is his.   EX 20:2-17

THE COMMANDS OF CHRIST:
You shall love the Lord your God
          with all your heart,
            all your soul,
            all your mind,
          and all your strength.
You shall love your neighbor as yourself.
There is no other commandment
     greater than these.   MK 12:30-31

A new commandment I give you:
Love one another as I have loved you,
that you love one another.   JN 13:34
If you love me,
you will keep my commandments.   JN 14:15

GOD:

Did I aim at righteousness, godliness, faith,
    love, steadfastness, gentleness?   I TIM 6:11
Did I strive for that holiness,
    without which no one will see God?   HEB 12:14
Did I flag in my zeal?   ROM 12:11
Did I serve the Lord?   ROM 12:11
Was I constant in prayer?   ROM 12:11

NEIGHBOR:

Did I strive to excel
    in building up the Church?   I COR 14:12
Did I strive to please my neighbor,
    for his good?   ROM 15:1, 2
Did I show perfect courtesy to all men?   TIT 3:1, 2
Do I love my enemies,
    do good to those who hate *me*,
    bless those who curse *me*,
    pray for those who abuse *me*?   LK 6:27
Have I let love be genuine?   ROM 12:9
Did I love with brotherly affection?   ROM 12:10
Did I practice hospitality?   ROM 12:13
Did I live peaceably with all?   ROM 12:18
Did I pass judgment on another?   ROM 14:13
Did I bear with the failings of the weak?   ROM 15:1
Was I kind to another?
    tenderhearted?
    forgiving?   EPH 4:32
Did I speak the truth to my neighbor?   EPH 4:25
Did I let the sun set on my anger?   EPH 4:26
Did I strive to bear another's burdens,
    and so fulfill the law of Christ?   GAL 6:2

Did I encourage the fainthearted?
    help the weak?
Was I patient with them?   I THESS 5:14
Did I fail to respect those who labor among us,
    in the Lord?   I THESS 5:12
Did I speak evil of anyone?   TIT 3:1
Did I avoid quarreling?   TIT 3:1
Did I remember those in prison?
    those who are ill-treated?   HEB 13:3
Did I turn my eyes from one who is poor?   SIR 4:4
Did I give to everyone who asked of me?   LK 6:30
Was I angry with my neighbor for any injury?   SIR 10:6
Did I forget a friend in my heart?   SIR 37:6

FAMILY:
Have I loved my wife as myself?   EPH 5:33
Have I loved my wife as Christ loved the Church?   EPH 5:25
Was I harsh with her?   COL 3:19
Did I live considerately with my wife?   I PET 3:7
Did I respect my husband?   EPH 5:33
Was my behavior reverent and chaste?   I PET 3:2

SELF:
Did I hate evil?
    Cling to what is good?   ROM 12:10
Did I commit a sin twice?   SIR 7:8
Am I ashamed to confess my sins?   SIR 4:26
Am I too confident of atonement?   SIR 5:5
Do I make a display of my wisdom?   SIR 10:26
Do I busy myself with many matters?   SIR 11:10

Do I find fault before I investigate?	SIR 11:7
Do I take my share of suffering?	2 TIM 2:3
Am I patient in tribulation?	ROM 12:12
Do I rejoice in hope?	ROM 12:12
Am I haughty? Conceited?	ROM 12:16
Do I seek to avenge myself?	ROM 12:19
Am I subject to governing authorities?	ROM 13:1
Do I conduct myself becomingly?	
No quarreling and jealousy?	ROM 13:13
Do I shun immorality?	1 COR 6:18
Do I take heed lest *I* fall?	1 COR 10:12
Do I seek to gratify the desires of the flesh?	GAL 5:16
Do I have an inordinate desire for luxury?	SIR 37:29
Do I give myself over to food?	SIR 37:29
Can I be called a slanderer?	SIR 5:14
Do I let evil talk come from my mouth?	EPH 4:29
Do I refrain from speaking at the proper time?	SIR 4:23
Whatever my task, *do I* work willingly?	COL 3:23
Do I do anything from selfishness or conceit?	PHIL 2:3
Am I ready for honest work?	TIT 3:1
Am I content with what *I* have?	HEB 13:5

PRAYERS OF REPENTANCE

WITH MOSES:

    The Lord is slow to anger,
        and rich in graciousness,
    forgiving faults and failure.   NUM 14:18
    The Lord is a God of tenderness
        and compassion,
        slow to anger,
        rich in kindness
        and in faithfulness;
    he maintains his kindness for thousands,
    forgiving fault and failure and sin.   EX 34:6-7

WITH JOB:

    Suppose I have sinned.
    What have I done to you,
    Tireless Watcher of men?
    Why should I be a burden to you?
    Can you not overlook my faults,
        or pardon my sins?   JOB 7:20-21

WITH SOLOMON:

    Hear from heaven,
    and forgive your servant's sins;
    forgive,
    and deal with each
    as his sin deserves,
    for you know the heart of each.   2 CHRON 6:27, 31

WITH ISAIAH:

    You guide the man of integrity,
        who keeps your ways in mind.

We have all withered like leaves,
blown by sins as by the wind.
No one called out your name,
or stirred himself to lay hold of you,
Do not let your anger go too far,
or think of our sins for ever.

IS 64:5-9

WITH BARUCH:
Lord, God of Israel,
a heart in anguish cries to you;
listen and take pity,
for we have sinned in your sight.
You are the Lord our God,
and we long to praise you.

BAR 3:1-3, 7

WITH DANIEL:
Lord, great God to be feared,
we have sinned,
we have done wrong,
we have acted foolishly,
we have disobeyed your commands.
Integrity is yours, Lord,
ours is the shame we bear.
To us the look of shame belongs,
to the Lord our God,
mercy and compassion.

DAN 9:5-9

WITH JONAH:
I am cast out from your sight.
How shall I ever look again
upon your holy Temple?

JON 2:5

WITH JEREMIAH:
> "Return, faithless sons,
>   I will heal your faithfulness!"
> We are here, we come to you,
> for you are the Lord our God.
> Truly, the hills are a delusion,
> as are the tumult of mountains.
> Truly, in the Lord our God
>   is Israel's salvation.   JER 3:22–23

WITH MICAH:
> What god can compare to you.
> Taking away our faults,
> pardoning our crimes,
> not cherishing your anger forever,
> delighting in showing mercy?
> Pity us once more,
> cast our sins down to the ocean floor,
> throw away all our sins.   MIC 7:18–19

WITH THE PRODIGAL SON:
> "Father, I have sinned
>   against heaven,
>   and against you;
> I no longer deserve
>   to be called your son;
> treat me at least like a servant."   LK 15:18–20

WITH PAUL:
> I am unspiritual;
> I have been sold to sin,
>   like a slave.
> I cannot understand my own actions.

I fail to do the things
    I want to do,
I do the very things
    I loathe to do.
I find nothing of good within me.
Within my soul
I dearly love God's law,
but my body follows
a different law.
Wretch that I am!
    Who will free me
    from this body that brings death?
Thanks be to God!
Jesus Christ our Lord!   ROM 7:14-25

WITH JOHN:
If we say:
    "There is no sin in us,"
we are fooling ourselves!
We are not facing reality!
But, if we acknowledge our sins,
then the faithful and just God
will forgive our sins
and cleanse us from everything
    that is wrong.
If anyone should sin
we have an advocate
    with the Father,
Jesus Christ, the just one;
he is the sacrifice
    that takes our sins away,
and not only ours,
    but the world's as well!   I JN 1:8, 2:1-2

THE CHURCH'S CONFESSION
OF ITS SINS

Justice is far from us,
righteousness keeps its distance.

We look for light, but find darkness!
    for brightness, but we walk in gloom!

We grope along the wall
    like the blind,
and feel our way,
    like those without sight!

We stumble at noon
    as though it were twilight,
and dwell in darkness
    like the dead.

We look for justice,
    but there is none,
    for salvation,
    but it is out of reach.

For our faults in your sight are many,
    our sins take the stand against us.
Yes, our sins are always with us,
    our wickedness always on our mind,
as we rebel and deny the Lord,
and turn our back on our God.   IS 59:9–13

FORGIVENESS FOR GOD'S PEOPLE

To the Lord our God
belong mercy and pardon,
because we have sinned against him,
and have paid no heed
to the voice of the Lord our God.

My God, listen, listen to us;
open your eyes,
and see our misery,
for we are not praying to you
relying on our own good deeds,
    but on your great mercy.
Lord, listen!
Lord, forgive!
Lord, pay heed,
    and act!
Without delay, Lord,
for your own sake, my God,
because your city
    and your people
are called by your name. Amen.   DAN 9:9, 18–19

A BRIEF PRAYER OF CONTRITION

I have committed a great sin.
But now I beg you, Lord,
to forgive your servant's fault,
for I have acted very foolishly.   2 SAM 24:10

THAT GOD PAY HEED TO OUR SORROW

Lord God of heaven,
    strong,
    great,
    inspiring awe,
keeping kindness and covenant
with those who love and obey you,
let your ears be listening,
and your eyes open,
to the prayer of your servant.
We have acted corruptly against you,
and have not kept the commandments,
    laws, and customs,
which you laid down
through your servant Moses.
Lord God,
let your ear pay attention
to the prayer of your servant,
and to the prayers of your servants,
who delight in revering your name. Amen.   NEH 1:5, 7 & 11

FOR DISTRESSED SOULS

Lord, look upon my distress:
my soul is in ferment,
my heart is wrung within me,
since I have been very rebellious.
Hear how I groan;
there is no one to console me.

All my enemies gloat over my troubles.
Let all their evil-doing come before you,
and deal with them,
as you have dealt with me for all my sins;
for my groans are many,
and I am sick at heart. LAM 1:20–22

A PRAYER FOR CORRECTION

You know, Lord,
that man is not master of his way;
man's course is not of his choosing,
nor is it he who directs his steps.

Correct me, Lord,
but in just measure!
Not in your anger,
lest you have me dwindle to nothing. JER 10:23–24

THAT GOD MAY BRING US BACK TO HIM

If our wrongs are witness against us,
then act, Lord, for your name's sake!
For our backslidings are many,
and we have sinned against you!

Hope of Israel, our Lord,
our Savior in time of trouble,
why are you like a stranger
    in our land,
like a traveler who only stays
    for a night?
Why are you like a man confused,
like a strong man powerless to save?
Yet you are in our midst, Lord,
and we are called by your name;
do not desert us!   JER 14:7–9

FOR CONVERSION OF ALL SINNERS

You, Lord, reign forever,
your throne stands from age to age.
Why, then, do you forget us forever?
Why do you forsake us for so long?
Make us come back to you, Lord,
and we will come back.
Give us back such days
as we had of old!
Or have you entirely rejected us,
with an anger that knows no limit?   LAM 5:19–22

A DIALOGUE OF REPENTANCE

You chastised me, and chastened I stand;
I was like an untamed calf.
If you will let me, I will come back,
    for you are the Lord, my God.
I turn in repentance;
I have come to my senses;
I strike my breast;
I blush with shame;
I bear the disgrace of my youth.

Often as I threaten him,
I still remember him favorably;
my heart still stirs for him.
I must show him mercy
    —says the Lord.

JER 31:18–20

HOPE FOR FUTURE FREEDOM FROM SIN

Grant me only these two things,
then I need not hide from your face:
    take away your hand, which holds me down,
    and no longer make me frightened of your terror.
Then call me, and I will answer,
or let me speak, and then you answer.
How many faults and failings have I?
Make me know my sins and misdeeds!
Why do you hide your face,
and consider me your enemy?

Will you chase a wind-blown leaf,
or pursue dried-up chaff?
For a tree there is always the hope
that it will sprout again when felled,
that its shoots can start life again.   JOB 13:20–25, 14:17

FOR A LIFE FILLED WITH GOOD

Lord, you have said:
Take your wrong-doing out of my sight.
May we
cease to do evil,
learn to do good,
search for what is right,
help the oppressed,
be kind to the orphan,
and plead for the widow;
for you have promised
though your sins are as scarlet
they shall be white as snow;
though they are as red as crimson,
they shall be like wool.   IS 1:16–20

THANKSGIVING FOR GOD'S FORGIVENESS

I give you thanks, Lord;
you were angry with me,
but your anger subsided,
and you gave me comfort.

See now,
God is my salvation!
I can trust and not be afraid,
for the Lord is my strength,
    my song,
and has become my salvation.   IS 12:1–2

PRAYER AFTER CONFESSION OF SINS

Lord, I called upon your name,
from the bottom of the pit;
you heard me pray,
"Do not close your ears
to my cry for help!"
You drew near when I called out to you,
and you said, "Do not be afraid!"
You have sided with my cause, Lord,
you have redeemed my life.   LAM 3:55–58

A PROMISE OF AMENDMENT

You, our God,
    are kind,
    loyal,
    patient,
    and govern all things
    with mercy.

Even if we sin,
    we are still yours,
since we acknowledge your power,
    but we will not sin,
since you acknowledge us as yours.

To know you is complete integrity;
to know your power—
this is the root of immortality.   WIS 15:1-3

A DOXOLOGY

This saying is sure
and worthy of full credence:
"Jesus Christ came into the world
to save sinners."

Among sinners I am foremost;
but mercy has been shown me
    for this reason,
that in me, the greatest sinner,
Jesus Christ may show
how perfectly patient he is,
and give an example
for eternal life
to all who will put faith in him.

To the King of ages,
deathless, unseen,
the only God,
    be honor
    and glory
forever and ever. Amen.   I TIM 1:15–17

7. Supplications

FOR FIRM FAITH AND CONFIDENCE

We pray
that the Word of the Lord
may speed on its way
and be triumphant;
that we may be rescued
from sinful, bigoted men;
for not everyone has the faith.

But *you*, Lord, are faithful
and will give *us* strength,
and will guard *us* from the evil one.

May *you*, Lord, turn our hearts
    to *your* love,
and to the steadfastness
that is Christ's. Amen.   2 THESS 3:1–5

FOR PERSEVERANCE IN FAITH

We are those who were called,
those dear to God the Father,
in the safe-keeping of Jesus Christ.

Grant us to build
    upon the foundation of faith,
to pray in the Holy Spirit,
and, keeping *our*selves
    in the love of Christ,
to wait for the mercy
of our Lord Jesus Christ,
who will give us endless life.

To him who is able to keep *us* from falling,
and present *us*,
guileless and joyful,
into his glorious presence,
to the only God,
who saves us through Jesus Christ our Lord,
be glory,
    majesty,
    authority, and
    power,
his for all time
and for ever. Amen.   JUDE 1:20-21, 24-25

ADHERENCE TO GOD'S WILL

Let the universe be disturbed
    by tempests from every quarter.

Let armed battalions
    close in deadly fray.

Let fleets be crippled
    and destroyed by fleets

Let the law courts ring
    with endless litigation;
and this is still
my chief business in life—
to conform myself entirely
to the one and only will of God.

And now I embrace,
and store within my heart,
that holy Word of God:
                            JEREMY DREXEL
and the world,
                    closing lines of Heliotropium
with all its cravings,
shall come to an end;
but whoever does the Will of God
will remain forever.   I JN 2:17

FOR THE GIFTS OF GOD

Every gift
that is good and perfect
is given us from above,
coming down
from the Father of lights.   JAS 1:16–17

Give me, Lord,
        purity of heart,
        heart clean and guileless,
        humility,
        fortitude, and
        patience.

Most high, undying WISDOM,
        drive from me the darkness
        and blindness of ignorance;

Most high, unfailing STRENGTH,
        deliver me;

Most high, undimming LIGHT,
        enlighten me;

Most high, unbounded MERCY,
        have mercy on me. Amen.   GALLICAN
SACRAMENTARY

THE PRESENCE OF CHRIST

May Christ live in *our* hearts,
through faith,
that deep-rooted and firm-grounded in love,
we will be able to grasp,
with all the saints,
the breadth and the length,
the depth and the height.   EPH 3:17-18

I adore you, Lord Jesus,
living within my heart,
and beg you to remain in me
in the quietness of your power,
in the perfection of all your ways,
in the brightness of your presence,
in the holiness of your Spirit,
that I may know the breadth,
     and length,
     and depth,
     and height of your love,
and trample down within me
all power of evil,
in the might of your Spirit,
to the glory of God the Father. Amen.   JEAN OLIER
                                          (ADAPTED)

FOR GROWTH IN CHRIST

Our Father
let love be genuine;
let us hate evil,
      and cling to what is good;
grant us
to love each other as brothers should,
to show profound esteem to each other.

Let us, never flagging in zeal,
      but with willing spirit,
      serve *you*, Lord.

Let us be joyful with hope,
      patient under stress,
      and constant in prayer.

Let us bless those who curse *us*,
      rejoice with those who rejoice,
      weep with those who weep,
      and show equal kindness to all.

Let us repay no one evil for evil,
but take thought of only
what will be honorable before all men.

Let us live peaccably with all men,
insofar as it is possible for *us*.
Through Christ our Lord. Amen.

ROM 12:9–18
(ADAPTED)

FOR GROWTH IN LOVE

I have come to set fire to the earth,
and how I wish it were already kindled.   LK 12:49

Inflame my soul
with the fire which you cast upon the earth,
and willed to be enkindled,
so that, with welling tears,
I may offer you daily
the sacrifice of an afflicted spirit
    and a contrite heart.   PS 50:1

Good Jesus,
since I long for,
and implore of you with all my soul,
grant me your chaste and holy love,
that it may fill me,
    hold me,
    and possess me fully. Amen.   ANON.

ONE'S FAMILY, ITS GROWTH IN LOVE

This is what I pray,
kneeling before the Father
    of our Lord Jesus Christ,
from whom every family,
    whether on earth or in heaven,
    takes its name:
Out of the richness of his glory,
may he give *us* the power,
    through his Holy Spirit,
to grow strong in our innermost being,
that Christ may dwell in *our* hearts by faith;
then, may *we*, deep-rooted and firm-grounded
    in love,
be able to grasp, with all God's people,
what is the breadth,
    the length,
    the depth,
    and the height
    of the love of Christ,
which surpasses knowledge;
and may *we* be filled
with all the fullness of God.

EPH 3:14–19
(ADAPTED)

FOR SELF-CONTROL

I pray
for a guard set over my mouth,
and prudence, to seal my lips,
to keep me from falling,
and my tongue from destroying me!

Lord, Father and Master of my life,
do not abandon me to their whims,
do not let me fall because of them.

Would that whips were set over my thoughts,
and wisdom, to discipline my heart,
to spare me when I make errors,
to let none of my sins go unchecked;
that my mistakes may not increase,
nor my sins see sins abound;
that I may not fall before my foes,
and have my enemies gloat over me!

Lord, Father and God of my life,
do not give me proud eyes,
turn lust away from me,
let no lust nor lechery rule me,
and do not hand me over to shame. Amen.   SIR 22:27–23:6

FOR A STEADFAST HEART

Come to me, all who labor
    and are over-laden,
and I will give you rest.
Take my yoke upon yourselves,
and learn from me,
for I am gentle and humble at heart,
and you will find rest for your souls.
For this yoke of mine lies easy,
this burden of mine is light.   MT 11:28–30

Lord, give me a steadfast heart,
which no unworthy affection
can drag downwards;
    an unconquered heart,
which no trial can wear out, and
    an upright heart,
which no untoward purpose
can tempt aside.
Bestow on me, Lord my God,
understanding—to know you,
diligence—to search for you,
wisdom—to find you, and
faithfulness—to finally embrace you. Amen.

ST. THOMAS AQUINAS

TO BE A SERVANT OF PEACE

Peacemakers, working for peace,
sow the seeds that will ripen into holiness.   JAS 3:18
Come, children, listen to me,
    I will teach you the fear of the Lord.
Which one of you desires life,
    and loves a life that prospers?
Keep your tongue from evil,
    your lips from speaking guile;
turn from evil, do good,
    seek peace, pursue it.   PS 34:12-15

Lord, make me an instrument of your peace!
Where there is hatred, let me sow love;
where there is injury, pardon;
where there is doubt, faith;
where there is despair, hope;
where there is darkness, light;
where there is sadness, joy.

Divine Master,
grant that I may not seek so much
to be consoled, as to console;
to be loved, as to love;
for it is in giving that we receive,
    in pardoning that we are pardoned,
    and in dying that we are born to eternal life.
ST. FRANCIS OF ASSISI

PRAYER OF ONE ENGAGED TO BE WED

Let us pray,
that the Lord may pity and protect us!

You are blessed, God of our fathers,
and blessed is your holy name,
glorious for ever!
Let the heavens bless you,
and all that you have made!

You made Adam,
and gave him Eve, his wife,
to be his help and support;
from them the race of man has sprung.

You have said,
"It is not good for man to be alone;
let us make a helper for him
          like himself."

And so, I do not take my sister (brother)
for any lustful purpose,
but I do so with sincerity.

Be kind, and grant us mercy,
that we may grow old together.
Amen! Amen!

TOB 8:5-8

PRAYER OF AN EXPECTANT MOTHER

Lord, who are over us,
grant your servant to pray to you;
    give us seed for our heart,
    and growth to our understanding,
so that fruit may be produced
by which every mortal,
    bearing the likeness of humankind,
may be able to love.
You alone *are*,
and we?—the work of your hands,
as you yourself have said.
You give life to the body,
    now fashioned in the womb,
and furnish it with members;
for nine months the womb,
    which you have formed,
endures the creation
which you have fashioned within.
But that which keeps,
and that which is kept,
are both placed in your keeping.
When the womb gives up again
what has been formed within it,
you have commanded
    that from the body itself
    milk should be supplied,
the fruit of the breasts,
so that what has been fashioned
may be nourished for a time,
and afterwards
you will guide him in your mercy. Amen.   AP 2 ESD 8:7–11

PRAYER OF PARENTS

It is always a great joy to me
to hear that my children live
according to the truth.

3 JN 4

Father of mankind,
help me fulfill my duty
towards these,
    your children,
    and mine.
Teach me what to give
    and what to withhold,
    when to reprove
    and when to forbear.
Make me gentle, yet firm,
    considerate, yet watchful,
neither weakly indulgent
nor excessively harsh.
Grant me to lead them
along true ways of holiness,
that with them I may share
in the unspeakable joys of our true home.

SOURCE UNKNOWN

PRAYER OF ONE WHO IS IN MOURNING

Lord God, Masterful King,
all things are in your power,
and no one can withstand you;
you have made heaven and earth,
and every wonderful thing
    under heaven,
for you are Lord of all,
and none can oppose your majesty;
Lord God, King,
    God of Abraham,
spare your people;
hear my prayer,
pity your inheritance.
Turn our mourning into feasting
    that we may live
    and sing our praises to your name.
    Amen.   ESTHER 1:9-12, 15-17

PRAYER OF A WIDOW

God, my God, hear me also—a widow.
You have made what has happened,
    what happens now,
    and what will follow;
you have planned what is and
    what will be.

What you designed has come to pass;
the things you have done
        presented themselves, saying,
        "Behold, we are here!"
For all your ways are planned ahead,
and your judgment is with fore-knowing.
You are the God of the lowly,
        help of the oppressed,
        strength of the weak,
        refuge of the lonely,
        salvation of the hopeless.
Hear me, God of my fathers, hear me!
        (Here a request may be added)
God of Israel's heritage,
Master of earth and heaven,
Maker of the oceans,
King of the whole creation,
hear my prayer! Amen.   JUDITH 9:4–12

FOR WATCHFULNESS

Let your belts be fastened
and your lamps ready to burn;
be like those
who wait the master's return from a wedding,
ready to open for him
as soon as he comes and knocks.   LK 12:35–36

Grant us by your grace, Lord,
that like the wise and watchful maidens,
who were ready by good works,
our way of life shall be watchful as well,
that we shall not sit in darkness,
    with darkened souls,
    in the mind's darkness,
but through prayer
we may ever look
on the shining splendor of your face
for ever. Amen.   st. ephraim

FOR CHRISTIAN WATCHFULNESS:
THE END OF OUR LIFE

If I asked darkness to cover me,
    and light to be night about me,
that darkness would not be darkness to you,
    that night would be like the light of day.   ps 139:11–12

Grant us, Lord,
to imitate the watchfulness
of those who waited
for your resurrection,
so that day and night, Lord,
our souls may be turned toward you.
In that hour when we shall be separated
from men, from the traffic of men,
be to us, Lord,
a Giver of good things;

bring joy to our sadness,
your peace into our hearts,
and your rest to all our striving,
that the darkness of that night
may be to us as day. Amen.   ST. EPHRAIM

DURING TIME OF TRIAL

My Lord, our only King,
help me,
for I am alone
and have no helper but you,
and danger is near at hand.
You are just, Lord!
Remember Lord,
make yourself known
in this time of our distress,
and give me courage,
    King of gods,
    Master of all dominion.
Save us by your own hand,
and help me,
for I am alone
and have no helper but you, Lord.
You know my need, God,
whose strength prevails
    over that of all others;
hear the voice of the despairing,
save us from the hands of sinners,
and save me from my fear!   ESTHER 14:3–19
(SHORTENED)

AT A TIME OF LOSS

Naked I came from my mother's womb,
naked shall I return;
the Lord gave, the Lord has taken back;
blessed be the name of the Lord. JOB 1:21

IN TIME OF GREAT CRISIS

Lord Almighty, Israel's God,
      the soul in anguish,
      the wearied soul
now cry out to you.
Hear, Lord, and have mercy,
for we have sinned in your sight!
You are enthroned forever;
we are perishing forever.
Almighty Lord, Israel's God,
hear now the prayer
      of Israel's dead,
      of the sons of those
      who sinned in your sight,
      who did not heed
      the voice of the Lord their God.
Therefore misfortune has clung to us.
Forget the sins of our fathers,
and in this time of crisis
remember your power
      and your name.

175

For you, Lord, are our God,
and you, Lord, we will praise.
You put reverence for you
    into our hearts,
that we should call on your name.   Bar 3:1–8

IN TIME OF TRIAL FOR THE CHURCH

Lord, why should your wrath
blaze up against your own people,
whom you brought out of Egypt
    with such awesome power
    and a mighty hand?
Remember Abraham,
    Isaac,
    and Jacob,
and how you swore to them
    by your own self, saying,
"I will give your descendants increase
as much as there are stars in the sky;
and all this land I promised,
I will give to your descendants;
they shall inherit it forever."   Ex 32:11–13

FOR THE RETURN OF ONE'S HEALTH

Heal me, Lord,
and I shall be healed;
save me,
and I shall be saved;
for you are my praise.
I have not urged you to send evil,
nor desired the day of misfortune;
you know this.
You know what passed my lips,
      it is present before you.
Be no terror to me,
you, my refuge in time of trouble.   JER 17:14, 16–17

BEFORE A JOURNEY

If I enjoy favor with you, Lord,
then come along in *my* company.
We are a headstrong people,
yet forgive our faults and our sins,
and take us for your heritage. Amen.   EX 34:9

FOR A GOOD END TO OUR LIVES

There still remains a seventh-day rest
for the people of God,
for whoever enters God's "Rest"
rests from his labors,
as God did from his.
Let us strive, then,
to enter that "Rest."　　　　　　　　　　HEB 4:9–11

Lord,
support us all the day long
of this troublous life,
until the shadows lengthen
　　　and the evening comes,
　　　and the busy world is hushed,
　　　and the fever of life is over,
　　　and our work is done.
Then, in your mercy,
grant us a safe lodging
　　　and a holy rest,
　　　and peace at the last. Amen.　　JOHN HENRY NEWMAN

THE HOUR OF JUDGMENT

Stay awake
for you do not know the day
when the Master is coming.
You may be certain
that if the owner of the house
had known at what time
the thief was coming,
he would not have allowed him
to break into the house.
You too must stand ready,
for the Son of Man is coming
at an hour you least expect.   MT 24:42–44

In that hour
when all who sleep
have put away their fleeting labors,
awaken in our souls, Lord,
the knowledge that does not deceive.

In that hour
when man's members
are clothed in burial linen,
clothe our inward man, Lord,
with your regeneration.

On that day
when all men are called to earthly burial,
make us worthy, Lord,
to rejoice in heavenly rest.

In that hour
when men shall cast from their bodies
the covering of night,
cast from our hearts, Lord,
the memory of perishing things.

In the morning
when sailors begin their labors at sea,
may our souls be at rest from all motion,
in your harbor.

In that hour
when all are set free
from the toils of this world,
grant us to rest, Lord,
in your unfading consolation.

In that day
when darkness shall cease,
and all are freed from weariness,
grant us to take delight, Lord,
in the joys of the life to come. Amen.   ST. EPHRAIM

FOR THE PROMISE OF HEAVEN

Lord God,
you have only begun to show your servant
    your greatness and your power;
for what "god" is there,
    in heaven or on earth,
who can do mighty deeds or works like you?
Let me go over, I pray,
and see that good land beyond the Jordan,
    that prosperous hill country,
    and Lebanon.   DEUT 3:24–25

8. *Prayers*

OUR FATHER

Our Father in heaven,
may your name be held holy,
  your kingdom come,
  your will be done
  on earth as in heaven.

Give us today the bread we need,
and forgive us our wrongs
as we forgive those who wrong us;
do not put us to the test,
but save us from the evil one. Amen.   MT 6:9–13

I BELIEVE

I believe   JN 9:38
   in God   TIT 3:6
   who calls into being
        things that do not exist,   ROM 4:17
   that he exists,
   and rewards those who search for him;   HEB 11:6
we know and believe the love God has for us.   I JN 4:16

I believe   JN 9:38
    in him whom he has sent   JN 6:29
    the Holy One of God,   JN 6:69
    Jesus our Lord
    who was put to death for our sins
    and raised up for our justification;   ROM 4:24
    that Jesus is the Christ,   I JN 5:1
    that Jesus is the Son of God,   I JN 5:5
    that Jesus died and rose again,   I THESS 4:14
    that God gives life to the dead   ROM 4:17
    and we shall live with him.   ROM 6:8
I believe   JN 9:38
    in the Truth,   2 THESS 2:13
    in the Light,   JN 12:36
    in the name of the only Son of God;   JN 3:18
I believe   JN 9:38
    everything laid down in the law
    or written in the prophets,   ACTS 24:14
    the word that Jesus spoke;   JN 4:50
Lord, I believe! Help my unbelief!   MK 9:24

A PRAYER OF FAITH

We keep our eyes fixed,
      not on things that are seen,
      but on things unseen;
      for things that are seen
          pass away,
      the things that are unseen
          outlast time.

For we are certain, *Lord*,
that when the frame that houses us
    is destroyed,
we have a house made by God,
    not by human hands,
that is eternal,
    in heaven.
Here, indeed, we groan,
longing to put on our heavenly home,
that by putting it on,
we might not go unclothed.

While we are still in our present state,
    we are anxious,
    we sigh;
not that we would go unclothed,
but that we would be further clothed,
    that what is mortal,
    may be covered over by life.

He who prepares us for this very thing
    is God,
    who gave us his Spirit as a pledge.
We always have faith, then,
we are convinced,
    that while we are "at home" in the body,
    we are away from the Lord,
    walking by faith, not by sight.
We are confident,
but would rather be away from the body,
    and "at home" with the Lord.   2 COR 5:1–8

AN EXPRESSION OF FAITH

Faith is the assurance of things hoped for,
the proof of things unseen.
By Faith we understand that the world
    was made by the Word of God;
By Faith Abel offered to God
    and was declared righteous;
By Faith Enoch was taken up
    and did not have to taste death;
By Faith Noah felt a holy fear
    and claimed the righteousness
    that comes of one's faith;
By Faith Abraham obeyed when he was called
    to go out to a country
    that he would receive as a heritage;
By Faith Sarah conceived
    even when she was past the age;
By Faith Abraham was willing
    to sacrifice his only son;
By Faith Isaac blessed Esau and Jacob
    for the distant future;
By Faith Moses left Egypt
    unafraid of the king's anger;
By Faith the people crossed the Red Sea,
    as though it were dry land;
By Faith the walls of Jericho fell;
By Faith Rahab was not killed
    along with the unbelievers.

With such a cloud of witnesses
on every side of us,
grant me to shrug every hindrance,
     and the sin that clings so easily,
     and to run in the race we have begun.
Let *me* never lose sight of Jesus,
     who leads us in our faith,
     and perfects it,
who, for the joy that was ahead of him,
     endured the cross,
     disregarding its shame,
and is seated at *your* right hand. *Amen.*   HEB 11:1–12:2
(SHORTENED)

A PRAYER OF HOPE

Blessed be the God and Father
of our Lord, Jesus Christ!
In his great mercy
he has given us a new birth as his sons,
by raising Jesus Christ from the dead,
so that we may have a certain hope,
     and the promise of a heritage
     that can never be spoilt or stained;   I PET 1:3–4

May we take a firm grip on the hope
     that is held out to us,
     which we have as a sure
     and steady anchor for the soul;   HEB 6:19

May we put on hope
    for a helmet of salvation; ɪ THESS 5:8
May we, by the examples the Scriptures give us,
    have hope; ROM 15:4
May we know Christ among *us*,
    the hope of glory; COL 3:27
    through him we have gained access
    to the state of grace,
    and look forward to sharing the glory of God; ROM 5:2
May it be my one hope,
    that I may never know defeat,
    but that now and always
    I may be able to have Christ glorified
    in my body, whether by life or death PHIL 1:20
for there is one Body, one Spirit,
    just as we were called into one hope. EPH 4:4
May the God of all hope
bring *us* such joy and peace
    in our faith,
that the power of the Holy Spirit
may grant an abundance of hope. *Amen.* ROM 15:13

A PRAYER OF LOVE

Show *me, Lord,*
the most excellent way of all.
I may be as eloquent as men or angels,
but without LOVE
    I am a noisy gong,
    or a clanging cymbal.

I may have the gift of prophecy,
knowing all mysteries, having all knowledge,
with a faith strong enough to move mountains,
but without LOVE,
    I am nothing.
I may give away all I have,
    even my body, to be burnt,
but without LOVE,
    I gain nothing.
LOVE is patient and kind;
LOVE is never jealous, nor boastful;
    is never conceited, nor rude;
LOVE never insists on its own way;
LOVE is not easily hurt, nor resentful;
    never gloats over evil,
    but rejoices in what is right;
LOVE bears all things, believes all things,
    hopes in all things, endures all things.
LOVE never ends:
    prophecies—they pass away;
    tongues—they will cease;
    knowledge—it too passes.
So faith, hope, love endure—these three;
but the greatest of these is LOVE.
Let me put LOVE first.   I COR 13:1–8, 14:1

BLESSING FOR ONE'S HOME

Lord God,
you are indeed God,
and your words are true.
May it please you, therefore,
to bless the house of your servant,
that it may always stand
    in your presence;
for you, Lord God, have spoken,
and with your blessing
shall your servant's house
stand blessed forever. Amen.   2 SAM 7:28–29

PRAISE TO GOD FOR HIS SAINTS

Alleluia!
Victory, glory, power to our God!
The fair Judge! The just Rewarder!
Praise our God, all you his servants,
all who revere him, great and small!
Alleluia!
The Lord our God, the Sovereign one,
    now reigns!
Let us be glad and be joyful,
and give him glory,
for the marriage of the Lamb has come,
and his Bride has made herself ready;

hers it is to be clothed in fine linen,
     pure and bright,
for the good deeds of the saints
is the finest of all linen. REV 19:2, 5, 7–9

IN PRAISE OF ALL THE SAINTS

A blessing on the poor in spirit,
     the kingdom of heaven is theirs.
A blessing on the gentle,
     they shall inherit the earth.
A blessing on those who mourn,
     they shall receive comfort.
A blessing on those
     who hunger and thirst for what is right,
     they shall receive their fill.
A blessing on the merciful,
     they shall obtain mercy themselves.
A blessing on the pure of heart,
     they shall see God.
A blessing on the peacemakers,
     they shall be called sons of God.
A blessing on those who suffer
for the cause of right,
     the kingdom of heaven is theirs. MT 5:3–10

THE SAINTS OF GOD

Do not let people
hold you in little regard;
but, be an example
to all the faithful
in the way you speak and act,
in your love,
    your faith, and
    your purity.   I TIM 4:12

Almighty, deathless God,
who kindled the flame of your love
in the hearts of your saints,
grant to us the same power
    of faith and love,
that, as we rejoice
    in their triumphs,
    we may profit
    by their examples.
Through Christ our Lord. Amen.   GOTHIC MISSAL

INVOCATIONS

OF FAITH IN CHRIST:

You truly are the Son of God!   MT 14:33

You are the Christ,
    the Son of the Living God!   MT 16:16

Rabbi, you are the Son of God!
    You are Israel's King!   JN 1:49

Rabbi, we know you are a teacher, sent by God;
    no one can do the signs you do
    unless God is with him!   JN 3:2

My Lord and my God!   JN 20:28

OF CONFIDENCE:

Lord, if you will it,
    you can make me clean!   LK 5:12

Father, if you will it,
    take this cup away from me;
    yet not my will, but yours be done.   LK 22:42

Stay with us, Lord, for it is almost evening,
    and the day is almost over.   LK 24:29

Jesus, remember me when you enter your Kingdom!
                                                                LK 23:42

FOR MERCY:

Save us, Lord, for we are perishing!   MT 8:25

Have mercy on us, Son of David!   MT 9:27

Lord, help me!   MT 15:25

Lord, be merciful to me a sinner!   LK 18:13

OF JOY:

A Blessing on one who will eat bread
    in the Kingdom of God!   LK 14:15

9. Intercessions

A GENERAL INTERCESSION—1

Scripture says,
"God opposes the proud,
but is generous to the humble."
Give in to God, then.
The nearer you come to God,
the nearer he will come to you.   JAS 4:7-9

We bring before you, Lord,
the troubles and perils
        of peoples and nations,
the sighing of prisoners,
the sorrows of the bereaved,
the needs of strangers,
the helplessness of the weak,
the hopelessness of the weary,
the failing powers of the aged.
Draw near to each, Lord,
for the sake of our Lord, Jesus Christ.
Amen.   ST. ANSELM

A GENERAL INTERCESSION—2

We prove we are God's servants
by our purity, knowledge,
    patience, kindness,
by a spirit of holiness,
by an unaffected love,
by the Word of truth,
and by the power of God.   2 COR 6:6-7

May the power of his mercy
strengthen our hearts in his truth.
May it confirm and calm our souls.
May his grace abound in us,
may he have pity on us,
and remove obstacles
from before us,
from before all who are dear to us, and
from before his holy Church.
May he, by his power,
    and abundance of his mercy,
enable us to please him forever,
through Jesus Christ his Son, our Lord.
Amen.   ST. AUGUSTINE

In every place, then,
I want men to lift up their hands
reverently in prayer,
with no anger or contention.   I TIM 2:8

Turning then to the Lord our God,
        the almighty Father,
in pureness of heart,
let us as best we can
give thanks with all our hearts;
beseeching him, that in his goodness,
he will graciously hear our prayers,
and by his power
drive evil from our thoughts
        and actions,
increase our faith,
guide our minds,
grant his holy inspirations,
and bring us to unending joy,
through his Son,
Our Lord and Savior,
Jesus, the Christ. Amen.   ST. AUGUSTINE

Father, the hour has come:
glorify your Son,
that your Son may glorify you;
through the power over all men
that you have given him,
let him give eternal life
to all whom you have given him.
Eternal life is this:
to know you
    as the only God,
and to know Jesus Christ
    as the One whom you have sent.   JN 17:1-3

Lord and Master, we beg you
to be our help and comfort.
Save those who are in trouble,
have mercy on the lonely,
lift up the fallen,
show yourself to the needy,
heal the ungodly,
convert the wanderers from your people,
feed the hungry,
raise up the weak,
comfort the faint-hearted,
let all the peoples know
that you are God alone
and Jesus Christ is your Son,
and we are your People,
    the sheep of your pasture,
for the sake of Jesus Christ. Amen.   ST. CLEMENT OF ROME

FOR THE FLOCK OF GOD

I myself will tend my flock,
I myself will watch over it.
I shall rescue them
from wherever they have been scattered . . .
I myself will pasture my sheep,
I will show them where to lie down.
I shall look for the lost one,
bring back the stray,
bandage the wounded,
and help make the weak ones strong.
I shall be a true shepherd to them.   EZEK 34:11, 15–16

Lord Jesus Christ,
Good Shepherd of the sheep,
who came to seek the lost,
and to gather them into your fold,
have compassion on those who
    have wandered from you;
feed the hungry ones,
cause the weary ones
    to lie down in green pastures,
care for those whose hearts are broken,
strengthen those who are weak,
that we, relying on your care
    and comforted by your love,
may abide in your guidance to our lives' end.
For your name's sake. Amen.   ANCIENT PRAYER
                                    (590 A.D.)

FOR ALL BAPTIZED INTO CHRIST

We are a chosen race,
a royal priesthood,
a nation set aside,
God's own people,
that *we* might sing
the praises of God,
who called *us* out of darkness
into his wonderful light.   I PET 2:9

Lord God, you have made all
who were reborn in Christ
a royal and a priestly race;
grant us both to desire
    and to be able to do
what you command,
that having called your people
to eternal life,
they may have one faith in their hearts,
and one law of love in their lives.
Through Christ our Lord. Amen.   GELASIAN
                                      SACRAMENTARY

FOR CHRISTIAN CONCORD

Teach us to mend *our* ways;
    to take *your* appeal to heart;

        to agree with each other;
        to be united in peace.
God of love and peace, be with *us*!   2 COR 13:11

200

FOR LOVE AMONG BROTHERS

The night is over,
the true light already shines!
Anyone who claims to be in the light,
but hates his brother,
is still in the dark.
But anyone who loves his brother
is living in the light,
and need have no fear of stumbling,
unlike the man who hates his brother
and is in the dark,
not knowing where he is heading,
since it is too dark to see.   I JN 2:8a–11

Lord God, who,
out of your great love for this world,
reconciled earth to heaven
through your only-begotten Son;
grant that we, who,
by the darkness of our sins,
are turned aside from brotherly love,
may, by your light shed into our souls,
be filled with your own tenderness
and embrace our friends in you,
and our enemies for your sake,
in a bond of mutual affection.   MOZARABIC LITURGY

FOR ALL WHO CALL ON THE NAME OF THE LORD

Our help is in the name of the Lord,
the Maker of heaven and earth. PS 124:8

God, Ruler of all things,
Father of the spirits,
and Lord of all flesh,
who has chosen our Lord Jesus Christ,
and us in him, to be his people,
grant to every soul of man
that calls on his glorious and holy name,
faith, fear,
peace, patience,
holiness and sobriety,
to be well-pleasing in his sight,
through our High Priest
        and Protector, Jesus Christ,
by whom be glory and majesty,
        honor and power,
now and forevermore. Amen. CLEMENT OF ROME

FOR THE WORLD'S CONVERSION

My heart's desire
is that they may be saved.
Scripture states:
"No one who believes in him
will have cause for shame,"

making no distinction
    between Jew and Gentile;
the same Lord
    is Lord of both,
and bestows his richness
    on all who call to him,
for "everyone who calls on the Lord
    will be saved."   ROM 10:1, 11–13

FOR LABORERS FOR GOD

Jesus went about through all towns and villages,
teaching in their synagogues,
proclaiming the Good News of the Kingdom,
and curing every kind of disease and sickness.
And when he saw the crowds,
he felt sorry for them
because they were dejected and harassed,
and like sheep without a shepherd.
So he said to his disciples,
"The harvest is plentiful,
but the laborers are scant;
ask the Lord of the harvest
to send laborers to his harvest."   MT 9:35–37

Lord God,
who wishes all men to be saved
and come to know the truth,
we pray you,
send laborers into your harvest,

and give them strength
to preach your Word with all boldness,
that your teaching may be welcomed and honored
throughout the world,
and that all nations may know you
as the true and only God,
and him whom you have sent,
Jesus Christ your Son, our Lord,
who lives and reigns with you
in the oneness of the Holy Spirit,
God forever and ever. Amen. ROMAN ORATION

FOR THOSE WHO PREACH GOD'S WORD

Lord,
enable your servants
to preach your Word
    with all boldness;
stretch your hand to heal
and cause signs
    and wonders to be done
in the name
of your holy Servant, Jesus. ACTS 4:29–30

FOR ONE'S CHILDREN

May the God
before whom my fathers Abraham and Isaac walked,
    the God
who has been my shepherd all my life till this day,
    the angel
who has delivered me from all evil,
bless *my* children;
in them let my name be preserved,
and the name of my fathers,
    Abraham and Isaac,
and may they grow in numbers
    on the earth.   GEN 48:15–16 (ADAPTED)

FOR ONE'S ENEMIES

You have heard how it was said,
"You shall love your neighbor,
and hate your enemy;"
but I say to you,
Love your enemies,
and pray for those who persecute you,
that you may be the sons
of your heavenly Father.   MT 5:43–44

I offer you
my prayers and intercessions
for those especially, who,
in any matter,
have hurt, grieved,
or found fault with me,
or who have done me any damage or displeasure;
for all those, whom,
at any time,
I have vexed, troubled,
burdened or scandalized,
by words or deeds,
knowingly or in ignorance.

Grant us all equal pardon for our sins,
and for our offenses against each other.
Take from our hearts, Lord,
all suspicion, indignation,
    wrath or contention,
and whatever will hurt charity
    and lessen love.

Have mercy on those
who crave your mercy,
give peace to them
that stand in need thereof,
and make us such as may be worthy
to enjoy your grace. Amen.   THOMAS Á KEMPIS

FOR THOSE IN AUTHORITY

God of our fathers,
Lord of mercy,
you made all things by your Word,
and in Wisdom you fashioned man
     to rule the creatures you have made,
     to govern the world in holiness
        and uprightness,
     and to render justice with integrity,
grant *them* WISDOM, that sits by your throne;
and reject *them* not from among your servants.
Send her from your holy heavens;
send her from your throne of splendor,
that she may be with *them*
     and work with *them*;
that *they* may learn what pleases you,
for she loves and fathoms all things.
She will guide *them* discreetly
     in all things,
and will guard *them* with her glory. *Amen.*   WIS 9:1–4, 10–11

FOR THE SICK

     Bless the Lord, my soul,
        all that is in me, bless his holy name!
     Bless the Lord, my soul,
        and remember all his kindnesses:
        he forgives all your offenses,
        he heals all your sicknesses.   PS 103:1–3

Lord, the Healer of all flesh,
who binds up wounds,
send a perfect healing from heaven
to all who lie on a bed of pain
within our city.
Turn their weakness into strength,
bless them with vigor of body,
restore them to perfect health,
and prolong their days
in happiness and well-being.
And let us say "Amen."   JEWISH PRAYER

FOR THE DEAD IN CHRIST

There was a rich man
who was dressed in purple and fine linen,
and who feasted well each day.
At his gate there was a poor man, named Lazarus,
who was covered with sores,
and longed to fill himself
with even the scraps from the rich man's table.
Even the dogs came and licked his sores.
Now the poor man died
and was carried away by angels
to the bosom of Abraham.   LK 16:19-22

By the merits of your Resurrection
from the dead,
Lord Christ,
let death no longer have dominion
over the faithful departed.
Grant to your servants,
we beg you,
a resting place in your dwelling,
and in the arms of Abraham.
Grant this to all who,
from Adam to this day,
have served you with a clean heart;
to our fathers and brothers,
to our friends and kindred.
Give a place in your heavenly kingdom, Lord,
to every man
who has done you faithful service
in his lifetime,
and to all, who,
in their fashion,
have striven toward you.   ANCIENT PRAYER

TO THE GOD OF PEACE

May the God of peace himself
make *us* entirely holy,
and may our spirit,
        and soul,
        and body
be kept sound and without shame

at the coming of our Lord,
    Jesus Christ; I THESS 5:23
May the peace of God
    which surpasses understanding,
keep *our* hearts and minds
in Christ Jesus; PHIL 4:7
May we be in agreement
    with one another,
    live in peace,
that the God of love and peace
    will be with us; 2 COR 13:11
May the Lord of peace
himself give *us* peace
    at all times,
    and in all ways! Amen. 2 THESS 3:16

A PRAYER FOR PEACE

Give peace to the land, LEV 26:6
peace on earth; LK 2:14
peace in the heights, JOB 2:52
peace in heaven; LK 19:38
peace like a river, IS 66:12
untroubled peace; PS 37:11
a universal peace,
    till the moon is no more, PS 72:7
a universal peace,
    for all who love your law; PS 119:165
a time of peace, ECCLES 3:8
peace to those who are far and near; IS 57:10

unbroken peace in this place,   JER 14:3
peace in this city;   JER 29:7
peace in full measure,   JER 33:6
peace to everyone who does good,   ROM 2:10
joy with those
    who give counsels of peace; PROV 12:20
peace which surpasses understanding,   PHIL 4:7
peace with all men.   HEB 12:14

PEACE IN OUR TIME

We bless the God of all,
who, in every way,
    does great things;
he exalts our days from birth,
and deals with us in his mercy.
May he give us cheerful hearts,
and bring us PEACE
    in our time,
as in Israel in times gone by.
May he entrust his mercy to us!
May he deliver us in our times!   SIR 50:22–24

10. Thanksgivings

FOR THE COMFORT OF GOD

Blessed be the God and Father
of our Lord, Jesus Christ,
the Father of gentleness,
and the God of all consolation,
who comforts us in all our sorrows,
that we in turn
might be able to give comfort
to those who are in any trouble,
with the very same comfort
by which we are comforted by God.

For, as we share abundantly
in the sufferings of Christ,
so too shall we share abundantly
in his comfort,
through Christ.   2 COR 1:3–5

FOR THE GREAT GIFT OF CHRIST

We thank you
God and Father,
who raised Jesus Christ from the dead,
that he sacrificed himself

for our sins,
to rescue us
from this present sinful age,
in accordance with *your* will,
our God and Father,
to whom be the glory
for ever and ever. Amen. GAL 1:3–5

FOR THE FIVE BLESSINGS IN CHRIST

Blessed be the God and Father
of our Lord Jesus Christ,
who has blessed us, in Christ,
with every spiritual blessing from heaven.
1. Even before the world was made
    you chose us to be in Christ,
    to be holy,
    to be blameless before him,
    and to be filled with love.
2. *You* destined us to become *your* sons,
    through Jesus Christ,
    for *your* own gracious purpose,
    that we might praise *your* glorious grace
        lavished so freely upon us
        in *your* Beloved,
3. in whom, through his blood,
    we have our freedom
    and the forgiveness of our sins,
    so rich is his grace,
    so freely showered upon us.

4. *You have* let us learn the mystery of *your* will,
with all wisdom and insight,
—that hidden plan set forth in Christ
from the beginning of time,
to be revealed in the fullness of time—
namely, to bring all things
under the headship of Christ,
whether things of earth or heaven.

5. And in him we were called as God's very own,
chosen, for *your* great glory,
to be the people that trusts in Christ
before he comes again.   EPH 1:3–12

FOR THE GOSPEL

Glory to him
who is able to make us strong enough
to live according to the Gospel,
and the proclamation of Jesus Christ,
the revelation of a mystery
kept secret for many ages,
but disclosed at last,
and through the writings of the prophets
made known to the nations
by command of the undying God,
to bring about the obedience of faith.
To God, who alone is wise,
be glory forevermore,
through Jesus Christ!   ROM 16:25–27 (ADAPTED)

FOR OUR CALL TO SALVATION

We give thanks,
    as we are bound to do,
to God, always,
because God chose *us*
    from the beginning
to be saved
    through sanctification by the Spirit,
    and through belief in the truth.
To this has he called *us*
through the gospel,
that we may obtain the glory
of our Lord Jesus Christ.
Now, may our Lord Jesus Christ himself,
    and God our Father
    who loved us
    and gave us eternal comfort,
    and the hope which grace brings,
comfort *our* hearts
and make them firm
in every good word and work. Amen.   2 THESS 2:13–14, 16–17

FOR OUR VOCATION AS CHRISTIANS

Thanks be to God, who,
wherever he goes,
always leads us about in triumph,
and through us,
spreads the fragrance of Christ everywhere.

We are truly the incense of Christ to God:
among those who are being saved
we are a fragrance that brings life.   2 COR 2:14–16

FOR THE GIFT OF FAITH

I thank you,
Father,
Lord of heaven and earth,
for hiding these things
from the learned and ingenious,
and revealing them to children.
Indeed, Father,
such was your gracious purpose.   MT 11:25–26

FOR FORGIVENESS

It is always in your power
to show great strength,
and who can withstand
the might of your arm?

In your sight the whole world
is but a speck of dust,
hardly tipping the scales!
—or like a drop of dew,
that falls to earth at morning!

But you are merciful to all,
and can do all things;
so you overlook men's sins,
that they may repent.

You love all the things that are,
and loathe nothing you have made,
for had you hated anything,
you would not have fashioned it.

How could anything continue to be
unless you had willed it?
—or be preserved,
unless you called it into being?

You spare all things,
for they are yours,
Lord and Lover of life,
whose deathless spirit
is in all things.

Therefore, little by little,
you correct those who offend you,
warning and reminding them
of the things whereby they sin,
that they may be rid of sinfulness,
and come to trust in you, Lord.   WIS 11:21–12:2

FOR FREEDOM FROM SIN

Sinful wretch that I am!
Who will rescue me
from this body, doomed to death?
Thanks be to *you*, God,
through Jesus Christ our Lord!
We who are in Christ Jesus
are not condemned,
because the law
      of the spirit of life
      in Christ Jesus,
has set *us* free from the law
      that brings sin
      and death!
For *you have* done
what the law,
      made ineffective through sins,
could not do;
You sent *your* only Son,
in the likeness of sinful flesh,
and in that flesh
he condemned sin.
This *you* did
in order that the law's command
might reach fulfillment in us,
who walk, not according to the flesh,
      but according to the Spirit!   ROM 7:24–8:4

FOR SUFFERINGS

Since, by faith,
we are judged righteous,
through Jesus Christ our Lord,
let us be at peace with *you*, God.
Since, by faith,
and through Jesus,
we have gained access
to this grace in which we stand,
we can take joy in the hope
of sharing glory with *you*, God.
More than that—
we take joy in our sufferings,
knowing that these sufferings
bring endurance,
and endurance brings character,
and character brings hope,
and hope can never disappoint us;
for, God, *your* love
has been poured into our hearts,
through the Holy Spirit,
which has been given us.   ROM 5:1-5

FOR FAVORS RECEIVED

The whole creation
was fashioned anew
in its nature,
complying with your commands,

so that your children
might be kept from harm.
Yes, Lord, in every way
you have made your people
great and glorious;
you have not failed to help them
at all times,
and in all places.   WIS 19:6, 22

FOR EVERLASTING LIFE

We shall not all die,
but we shall all be changed,
    in a moment,
    in the twinkling of an eye,
    at the sound of a trumpet.
The trumpet will sound,
and the dead will be raised—
    but imperishable—
    and we shall all be changed!
Our present perishable nature
must put on imperishability,
this mortal nature of ours
must put on immortality.
When this perishable nature
shall have put on imperishability,
and this mortal nature
its immortality,
then the Scriptures will be fulfilled,
which say:

221

"Death is swallowed up in victory!
Death, where is your victory now?
Death, where, now, is your sting?"
Death's sting is sin,
and sin's power is the law;
but thanks be to God,
who gives us the victory
through Jesus Christ, our Lord.   I COR 15:51-57

THE THANKSGIVING OF DAVID

May you be blessed,
Lord, God of Israel our father,
for ever and ever!
Yours, Lord, is greatness,
                power,
                splendor,
                unending days,
            and glory,
for everything in heaven and earth
is yours.
Yours, Lord, is the sovereignty;
you are above all things, supreme!
Riches and honor are your attendants,
you are the ruler of all,
and in your hand are strength and power;
it is within your hand
to give strength and greatness to all.
Now, our God, we give you thanks,
and praise the grandeur of your name.
Amen.   I CHRON 29:10-14

FROM THE PSALTER

Alleluia!
Praise God in his holy Temple!
Praise him, in heaven enthroned!
Praise him for his mighty wonders!
Praise him for his sovereign power!
Praise him with the blasting trumpet!
Praise him with the lyre and harp!
Praise him with drums and dancing!
Praise him the strings and pipe!
Praise him with the clanging cymbals!
Praise him with the cymbals' clash!
Let everything that has breath
    praise the Lord!
Alleluia!   PS 150

Your love, Lord, reaches to the mountains,
    your faithfulness to the clouds;
Your uprightness is like the high mountains,
    your judgments like the mighty deep.

Lord, guardian of man and beast,
    God, how precious is your love!
Therefore the sons of men
    take refuge in the shadow of your wings.
They feast on the fullness your house affords,
    you give them drink from the font of pleasure;
Indeed, with you is the fountain of full life,
    and by your light we see light.

Never stop loving those who love you,
    or being righteous with upright hearts.
                                        PS 36:5-10

I thank you, Lord, with all my heart,
    for you have heard all I said.
In the sight of angels I sing to you,
    and bow low towards your holy Temple.

I thank your name for your faithful love,
    for you made your promise greater than your name.
When I called to you, you answered me,
    and made my soul wax strong.

Lord, all the kings on earth give you thanks,
    for they have heard of your promises.
They feast the Lord's great deeds,
    "Great is the glory of the Lord!"

From far above the Lord sees the lowly,
    but from far away he marks the proud.
Though I am ever in distress,
    you keep me alive, infuriate my foes.

You stretch out your hand and keep me safe,
    your right hand does all things for me.
Lord, your love is an endless thing,
    do not forsake us, whom you have formed.   PS 138